Essays on Biblical Counseling
Volume 4

COUNSELING AND THE SOVEREIGNTY OF GOD

AND OTHER ESSAYS

Jay E. Adams

Institute for Nouthetic Studies, a ministry of Mid-America Baptist Theological Seminary, 2095 Appling Road, Cordova, TN 38016
mabts.edu and nouthetic.org

Counseling and the Sovereignty of God: Essays on Biblical Counseling, Volume 4
by Jay E. Adams
Copyright © 2025 by the Institute for Nouthetic Studies,

New Testament quotations are from the Christian Counselor's New Testament and Proverbs Copyright © 2019 by the Institute for Nouthetic Studies. © 1977, 1980, 1994, 2000 by Jay E. Adams

ISBN: 978-1-949737-78-3 (Print)
ISBN: 978-1-949737-79-0 (Ebook)

Editor: Donn R. Arms
Design: James Wendorf | www.FaithfulLifePublishers.com

Library of Congress Cataloging-in-Publication Data
Names: Adams, Jay E., 1929 - 2020

Title: *Counseling and the Sovereignty of God, Essays on Biblical Counseling, Volume 4* Jay E. Adams
Description: Cordova: Institute for Nouthetic Studies, 2025
Identifiers: ISBN 9781949737783 (paper)
Classification: LCC BV4012.2.A4 | DDC 253.5

All rights reserved. No part of this publication may be reproduced, stored in a retrieval system, or transmitted in any form or by any means – electronic, mechanical, photocopy, recording, or any other – except for brief quotations in printed reviews, without prior permission of the publisher.

Published in the United States of America

Table of Contents

Foreword

Counseling and the Sovereignty of God	1
A Certain Inheritance	15
Counseling and the Five Points of Calvinism	27
Counseling the Unbeliever	43
The Influence of Westminster	63
The Biblical Perspectives on the Mind-Body Problem	71
Biblical Counseling and Practical Calvinism	111
Design for a Theological Seminary	119
Issues of the Heart	131
Theology Today	139
On Writing	145
Influence	153

Foreword

Jay Adams believed that at the core of every counseling problem was a theological problem. He wrote extensively about the theological issues that under-girded good counseling and warned about the devastating effects of bad theology. In addition to his books that focused on theology,[1] he contributed theological essays to a number of journals, festschrifts, and blogs. Most of the articles in this collection deal with theology and will be a help to any believer, but especially to the biblical counselor.

The title article, Counseling and the Sovereignty of God, deals with the single most important theological issue for the counselor. Counselors who do not have a firm understanding of this key doctrine will founder in the counselor room and will leave their counselees confused and without hope. In the concluding article, Influence, Dr. Adams warned the founding fathers of the National Association of Nouthetic Counselors (NANC)[2] to be on guard about many of the issues we continue to face over half a century years later.

My prayer is that you will profit from this collection from one of God's unique servants as much as I have editing it.

Donn R. Arms, editor

---

[1] Theology of Counseling, How to Help People Change, Sanctification and Counseling, The Importance of Faith in Counseling.
[2] Now the Association of Certified Biblical Counselors (ACBC).

Counseling and the Sovereignty of God[1]

A fourteen-year-old girl is abducted by a married man, the father of three children, who carries her off to an unknown destination. During the horror of the uncertain days that follow, what can sustain her parents? What is the supreme fact to which the Christian counselor can appeal that will bring hope and some measure of relief?

A family of seven, barely scraping along on the meager salary of a blue-collar worker in this inflationary era, is suddenly plunged into disaster by the closing down of the plant at which he works and his inability to obtain other work. They face the problem of survival amidst the uncertainties of a volatile world economy poorly managed by greedy and godless men. On what basis do they try to go on? Is there any use? Is there any meaning to it all? Any hope? To help them understand and cope with this dilemma, what does their pastor tell them? To what bottom-line truth should he point?

There is but one—the sovereignty of God.

Knowing that God knows, that God cares, that God hears their prayers, and that God can and will act in His time and way to work even in this for good to His own—*that*, and nothing less than that conviction, can carry them through. And what that hope may be reduced to is a confident assurance that God is sovereign.

It has always been so.

When the problem of evil burned like an inextinguishable fire in his bones, and in the frustration of his situation, he cried for a personal hearing before God in order to vindicate himself and discover why he

---

[1] This lecture was delivered at Westminster Theological Seminary, October 10, 1975 on the occasion of Dr. Adams' inauguration as Professor of Practical Theology.

had become the object of such pain and sorrow, Job received one answer and one alone. From out of the whirlwind came the final unequivocal Word to be spoken concerning human suffering:

> *I do in all the world according to my own good pleasure. I scattered the stars in the sky as I saw fit, and I created the beasts of the field and stream according to my desires. Job—where were you when all this took place? And who are you to question what I do with my own? I am sovereign.*

In discussing the outcome of the remarkable course of history, that through slavery and temptation and imprisonment at length raised him to the second highest political position in the world, Joseph assured his brothers: "You did not send me here, but God did" (Genesis 45:8). And in a further affirmation, that was destined to become the Romans 8:28 of the Old Testament, he declared: You planned evil against me, but God planned it for good (Genesis 50:20). His firm conviction of this truth, doubtless growing stronger throughout the span of those hard days, was what made it all endurable.

When Moses protested that he could not undertake the task to which God was calling because of his slowness of speech, God did not acquiesce, argue, or plead. He simply asserted His sovereignty in powerful words by means of a stinging statement: "Who made man's mouth?" (Exodus 4:11).

Under the most extreme sort of pressure to engage in idolatrous worship, Shadrach, Meshach, and Abednego (according to the words of their unflinching testimony) rested solely upon the sovereignty of God: "Our God," they said, "is able to deliver us" (Daniel 3:17). And true to their word, in what may have been a pre-incarnate Christophany, that God in sovereign loving care walked through the fire with them.

In addition to these, others, who endured taunts and blows, fetters and prison, who were stoned to death, tortured, sawed in two, run through with the sword—others, I say, in faith rested upon the promises of a sovereign God whose Word they believed to be true and whose promise they considered to be unfailing. The threat of death itself was not enough to shake their confidence in a *sovereign* God.

Yes, it has always been that way; the sovereignty of God is the ultimate truth that meets human need. That is why the pastoral counselor, above all men, must believe this truth and search out its implications for each and every counseling situation.

That is why today, in the midst of the many modern crises that individuals and families undergo, the pastoral counselor who most assuredly affirms the sovereignty of God will bring the most significant help of all. Freudian fatalism, Rogerian humanism, and Skinnerian evolutionary theory all fall woefully short of this help. Nothing less than this great truth can satisfy the longing heart or calm the troubled soul.

That is the way that it always has been, and this is the way that it always will be.

A counselor's theology and his use of it in counseling, then, is neither a matter of indifference nor a question of insignificance. Rather, it is an issue of the most profound importance. Truth and godliness, the reality of God, and the welfare of His people are inseparable. The godly man who copes with life is always the one who has appropriated God's truth for his life.

Take, for instance, the question on the lips of nearly every counselee—Why? Why did *this* have to happen? Why did it have to happen to *me*? Why did it have to happen *now*? Why? Why? Why?

Evolutionary explanations do not satisfy; they only aggravate. If man is no more than an animal, what hope is there? And of what significance is any attempt to change? The only value is the preservation of the herd.

Deistic determinism is no better. According to those who espouse such views, suffering merely follows as the inevitable consequence of the onward motion of impersonal law, in which the plight of the individual does not touch the heart of God since He has safely distanced Himself from His creation.

Existential embarrassment over the equivocation of a call to an authentic acknowledgment of the *absurd* can do no more than increase the pain.

Arminian answers that intimate that the problem may be a cause of frustration to God as well as to the counselee serve only to point the discouraged, defeated disciple to a pathway that leads ultimately to atheism.

The only explanation that can fully set to rest this insistent human inquiry into the ultimate reason for the existence of misery and death is that the all-powerful God who created and sustains this universe for His own good ends sovereignly has decreed it.

By this reply, simultaneously are swept aside all notions of man in the clutches of a blind, impersonal force, every concept of a weak and unworthy deity who is to be pitied along with the rest of us because He can control His runaway world no longer, and any lingering suspicion that the destiny of a human being is nothing more than a move in a cosmic chess game in which he is as ruthlessly dispensed with as if he were a pawn—heedless of the welfare of any other piece than the King. He *is* sovereign; all *does* exist for the King. But this kingly God of creation plays the game according to His own rules. He is altogether sovereign and, therefore, the Originator of the game as well—rules and all. And as He faultlessly makes each move across the board, His strategy for winning the game involves the blessing of His loyal subjects as well as His own glory. And each subject, whose every hair is numbered, moves as He moves in a responsible manner that He has sovereignly ordained.

So, you can see that a firm dependence upon the sovereignty of God is a dynamic concept in counseling—one that makes a difference, *the* difference—and, therefore, one that must under-gird every effort at counseling. If, indeed, God is sovereign, ultimately all turns out well. All problems have solutions; every blighting effect of evil will be erased and all wrongs righted. The counselor who knows God as sovereign has found fertile ground in which to plant his pastoral ministry. He will soon send down a taproot through which he will draw the living waters of life for many thirsty souls. Rooted and grounded in this foundational doctrine, his standpoint allows him the freedom to view and evaluate both the grand sweep of things and the plight of a poor sinner agonizing in the throes of personal grief. The sovereignty of God is the ground of hope and order in all that he does in counseling. It is the basis for all assurance that God's scriptural promises hold true. It is the cornerstone of Christian counseling.

But, before going any further, let me warn against two distinct but dangerous tendencies of those who, while superficially holding the truth of the sovereignty of God, draw faulty implications from that great teaching. The biblical doctrine lends no support whatever either to those who, with near profanity, so glibly cry, "Praise the Lord, anyway" in all sorts of inappropriate situations, nor does it provide comfort for mechanistic fatalists who wish to discount the idea of personal responsibility before God.

Taking the first matter seriously, there are at least two things to be said. On the one hand, counselors must clearly affirm that sin exists and—along with it—that "misery" of which the catechisms so meaningfully speak. There can be no Christian Science-like denial of the stark tragedy of human existence since Adam. There can be no facile self-deception aimed at alleviating misery by attempting to conceal its true nature beneath a heap of pious expletives, symbolized in the phrase "Praise the Lord, anyway." This vain effort, in the end, only lets one down hard. The counselor must give full recognition to sin and its terrifying effects if he wishes to be a faithful minister of the Lord Christ. After all, the Man of *Sorrows*, who was acquainted with *grief*, also believed in the sovereignty of God. Yet, He wept.

On the other hand, with equal vigor, every counselor worthy of the name of Christ must impress upon his counselees the truth that the existence of a sovereign God is truly a cause for great joy and hope in the midst of tragedy and sorrow. For if God is sovereign, life is not absurd; it has design, meaning, and purpose.

Unlike existentialists, who vainly try to find meaning in man himself, the Christian pastoral counselor will show that this misdirected humanistic viewpoint is what constitutes the unbearable *angst* of which they so powerfully speak. Instead, the counselor directs the counselee's attention from creatures who, in Adam, have done little better than to get themselves involved in a kind of global Watergate affair before God. It is to the sovereign Creator and Sustainer of the universe, rather than to fallen creatures, that he bids counselees to look for the final explanation that he seeks.

Apart from such a God, who knows the end from the beginning (because He ordained it), human beings cannot explain their existence because they have no eschatology; death ends all. But, in Him, there is a *denouement*. There will be an ultimate disclosure of the unrevealed particulars of His divine purpose. Those things that now so often seem to be meaningless functions in the course of human activity will all come alive with significance. Each piece of the puzzle at last will be put in place—the dark purples of despair, the fiery reds of anger and affliction, the sickly yellows—and we shall be permitted to view the whole as it now exists in the plan of God alone. The comforting conviction that there is a beautiful, meaningful picture on the cover of life's puzzle box, to which each piece of distress and pain bears a faithful resemblance, belongs solely to those who affirm the sovereignty of God. Without such a conviction, there is no hope.

Likewise, one can escape the fear of a disorderly world, relentlessly rolling on like an avalanche that is out of control, only by adhering to the doctrine of the sovereignty of God. Because of the certainty of order and control that the doctrine requires, even crazy and bizarre behavior in human beings is not inexplicable to the Christian counselor. Behind its baffling facade lies an etiology that can be traced immediately to personal rebellion against God and His laws, or (as a physiological consequence of Adam's sin) may extend all the way back to Eden. Either way, he knows that deviant human thought and action are not the result of mere chance. It is explicable in terms of a violated covenant and the judgment of a personal God.

Thus, hope wells up in the heart of every man to whom God reveals Himself savingly, for there is One who came to pay the penalty for the broken law and to keep covenant with the Father. Because of His perfect fulfillment of all that God demands, men may be saved here and hereafter from the penalty and from the grip of sin. Ultimately, the evil consequences of sin will be removed altogether from the lives and from the environment of the redeemed. Indeed, so great will be the effects of salvation that those who were created lower than the angels will in Christ be raised far above by His grace. They will share with Him in His glory. So, you see, there is meaning in it all, after all. Where sin abounded, grace more fully abounds. Even the absurd and the bizarre take on meaning as the foil against which the glory of God's grace may best be displayed.

And, lastly, there is hope also in the fact of God's sovereignty because His is a personal rule over His subjects. The atonement, by which the redeemed were reconciled to God, was no impersonal or abstract transaction, as if Christ died for "mankind." He is a *personal* Savior who loved particular individuals and shed His blood for them.

Cicero, in *De Natura Deorum* (2:66), wrote: "Magna dei curant, parva neglegunt." ("The gods are concerned with important things; trifles they ignore.") No such God is the sovereign God of our salvation. A sick child was of no consequence to Venus or Aphrodite. Larger questions—like some of the ongoing rivalries and disputes with the other gods and goddesses of the Greek and Roman pantheons—occupied their time and attention. Such gods brought no comfort or hope to men, because they were not sovereign. Much of creation slipped by beyond their purview.

But there is hope in the presence of the true Sovereign because He is in control of everything. Not a sparrow falls without Him. He is the God of trifles. Jesus taught us by His works and words what this sovereign God is like. The way that He put it was: "He who has seen me has seen the Father."

And, it is in that very Gospel of John in which these words are recorded that we are so pointedly shown Jesus' deep concern for individuals—Nicodemus, the woman at the well, the blind man, Lazarus, Mary and Martha. It is in the same Gospel that we hear Him speak of His shepherdly concern, a concern that extends to the hundredth sheep and that calls each by name. The sovereign Shepherd of Israel is great enough to care about trifles—like us. He labors under none of the limitations of the classical gods. Nor does He stand at a deistic distance in disinterest. This sovereign God is the father of a redeemed family over which He exercises total care and concern. There is plenty of hope for every Christian counselor in that.

Moving now along a continuum full of factors that might command our attention, I suggest that we pause for a moment to urge every pastoral counselor to remember the sobering fact that the existence of a God who is sovereign neither removes nor lessens, but (rather) *establishes* human responsibility to that God. If He who is sovereign over all men and over all their actions has determined that they shall be responsible to Him—then that settles it. That is how it is when a sovereign Creator speaks. It does not matter whether it is difficult to reconcile responsibility with sovereignty or not, because that is precisely what God decreed: Men shall be responsible to Him! And if He sovereignly determined to create man as a being fashioned in His image and governed by His moral law, so be it! That is the prerogative of a sovereign God.

Shall the pot say to the potter, "Why have you made me thus?" When you stop to think about it, to whom could one be more responsible than to the One who created him and sustains his every breath? To put it another way—because God is sovereign, He is the *only* one who is not responsible to another. Did not the Lamb of God Himself, who according to the sovereign plan of God was "slain from the foundation of the world," nevertheless declare, "It is proper for us to fulfill all righteousness"?

That statement presupposes responsibility.

It should be eminently clear, then, that God's sovereignty neither encourages the utterance of pietistic platitudes like "Praise the Lord, anyway" as the solution to the problem of human suffering, nor does it leave us unaccountable. Indeed, it is this very truth that *demands* of us nothing less than a realistic, eyes-wide-open response to the existential situations of life, for God will hold us answerable both as counselors and counselees.

All counseling that measures up to the biblical standard must fully acknowledge both the tragedy of sin and the fact of human responsibility; it must reckon with God's ultimate purpose to glorify Himself in His Son and in a people redeemed by His grace. While all things will turn out well, they do so, not apart from but precisely because of the responsible action of the Son of God, who came and actually died for those who, from all eternity, had been ordained to eternal life.

It should be obvious that I have not attempted to open up the many practical implications of the doctrine of God's sovereignty in any concrete way. The doctrine is so foundational that the number of such implications is large. I wish rather to invite you to join me in extracting the ore from this virtually untouched mine.

The sovereignty of God has been taught and preached largely in an abstract way—but little has been done to explore the applications of this doctrine for life and (therefore) for counseling. Moreover, Christian counseling has failed to measure up to its name principally because its early theorists were unskilled in exegesis and theology. They came to counseling mainly from a background in psychology. Yet, as important as psychology (rightly conceived and practiced) may be, it can never be foundational to counseling; it can only be ancillary.

Counseling—as we shall see—has to do with the counselee's relationship to persons. God and all the others who people his horizon are its concern. Only incidentally does the counselor concern himself with other matters. Clearly, love for God and one's neighbor is a prime interest of the minister of the Word.

That is why, here at Westminster Theological Seminary over the past ten years, the attempt has been made to teach pastoral counseling from the starting point of God's sovereignty. In everything that has been done and every word that has been written, it has been our goal to take that doctrine seriously, following its implications obediently, no matter where they might lead. Often the road has proven both difficult and unpopular, yet travel along it has always been satisfying. Temptations to veer to the right or to the left have been numerous. It has not always been easy to resist them. God alone knows how well we have succeeded in doing so.

"But," you inquire, "can you tell me more about the ways in which the doctrine of God's sovereignty has affected the theory and practice of the teaching of counseling at Westminster?" The basic answer to your question is this: Both theory and practice have been affected in *every* way.

But to become more concrete, let me mention what I consider to be the most significant influence the doctrine has exerted, an influence that has had a marked effect on both theory and practice. Early in the development of a counseling stance from which to teach, the question of encyclopedia arose. To what task does the pastoral counselor address himself? In counseling, does he handle a very narrow band of "spiritual" or "ecclesiastical" problems, or is his field of legitimate activity substantially larger? Is his counseling activity bordered (and thereby limited) by others from clearly distinct disciplines, namely psychologists and psychiatrists (whose titles, curiously enough, might be translated—not too freely—as "soul specialists" and "soul healers")?

Over the years, the question has always been kept in view. Gradually, the Scriptures have driven us to an answer, an answer that one hardly would have chosen by himself. The conviction has grown that it is God's answer. And when God speaks by His inerrant Word, what He says is *sovereign*.

Because of the teaching of the Scriptures, one is forced to conclude that much of clinical and counseling psychology, as well as most of psychiatry, has been carried on without license from God and in autonomous rebellion against Him. This was inevitable because the Word of the sovereign God of creation has been ignored.

In that Word are "all things pertaining to life and godliness." By it, the man of God "may be fully equipped for every good work." And it is that Word—and only that Word—that can tell a poor sinner how to love God with all of the heart, and mind, and soul, and how to love a neighbor with the same depth of concern that he exhibits toward himself. All the laws and prophets hang on these two commandments. They are the very summation of God's message to the world and to His redeemed people. As a consequence, it is the calling of the shepherds of God's flock (par excellence) to guide the sheep into the pathways of loving righteousness for His Name's sake. Putting it that way—that God's Name is at stake—shows the importance of this task.

"All of that sounds quite biblical, and it all sounds very innocuous," you may say. "But," you continue, "I don't see where that puts psychologists and psychiatrists in conflict with God. You'd better explain that one more fully." OK. Let me screw the two things together for you so that you can see the interconnection that leads to the conflict.

In assigning the pastor the task of helping sheep learn how to love God and neighbor, God has spoken sovereignly. If this is the pastor's task, clearly delineated in the Bible, then he must pursue it. This puts him in the counseling business. But, immediately, upon surveillance of the field, he discovers all sorts of other persons already out there trying to do similar things and saying that to them, not to him, belongs the task of counseling. There are competitors in the vicinity. Indeed, even a cursory investigation indicates that they are not merely in the vicinity but in the sheepfold itself. And as a result, the true shepherd soon discovers that they are leading the sheep astray.

"But," you ask, "is there no basic difference between the work done by psychologists and psychiatrists and that done by a pastor?" There is no way to distinguish between the work of the pastor as it is sovereignly ordered in the Scriptures and that which is attempted by others who lay claim to the field. People who come to counselors for help are people who are having difficulty with people. They don't come complaining, "You see, I've got this problem with my carburetor." That is why love for God (*the* Person) and for one's neighbor are such vital factors in counseling. Nothing could be more central to a pastor's concern. Yet, it is with this concern about persons that psychologists and psychiatrists also busy themselves. They want to change persons and the relationships between persons.

I contend, therefore, that it is not the pastor who is responsible for the overlap; it is the psychologist on the one side, who has moved his fence over onto the pastor's territory, and the psychiatrist on the other, who also has encroached upon his property. Unfortunately, until recently, pastors have been all too willing to allow others to cut their grass. At long last, largely under the impetus of Nouthetic counseling, there has been a noticeable change in attitude by conservative pastors everywhere.

"Now, wait a minute. Are you saying that psychology and psychiatry are illegitimate disciplines? Do you think that they have no place at all?"

No, you misunderstand me. It is exactly not that. Remember, I said clearly that they live next door to the pastor. My problem with them is that they refuse to stay on their own property. I have been trying to get the pastor to mow his lawn to the very borders of this plot.

Psychology should be a legitimate and very useful neighbor to the pastor. Psychologists may conduct many helpful studies of man (e.g., on the effects of sleep loss). But psychologists—with neither warrant nor standard from God by which to do so—should get out of the business of trying to change persons. Psychology may be descriptive, but it transgresses its boundaries whenever it becomes prescriptive. It can tell us many things about what man does, but not about what he should do.

Similarly, the neighbor who lives on the other side of the pastor's lot could be a most welcome one with whom the pastor could live in real harmony were he satisfied to play croquet in his own yard. Psychiatrists, for the most part, are a tragic lot. I say this not only because among the professions, psychiatrists have the highest suicide rate, but more fundamentally because they are persons highly trained in skills that they hardly use and instead spend most of their time doing what they were never adequately trained to do. In the United States, psychiatrists are physicians who (for the most part) use their medical training to do little else than prescribe pills. Freud himself acknowledged that a background in medicine is not required for the practice of psychiatry. That is why, in other parts of the world, psychiatrists are not necessarily medical persons. And that is why clinical and counseling psychologists do the same things as psychiatrists without specialized training as physicians.

The pastor recognizes the effects of Adam's sin upon the body; he, therefore, has no problem working side-by-side with a physician who treats the counselee's body as he counsels him about its proper use. From the days of Paul and Luke, pastors have found kinship with medical personnel. Why, then, does the psychiatrist present a problem? Certainly, it is not because of his medical background. The problem is that he will not stay in his own backyard. He keeps setting up his lawn chairs and moving his picnic table onto the pastor's property.

If he were to use his medical training to find medical solutions to the truly organic difficulties that affect attitudes and behavior, the pastor would be excited about his work. But the difficulty arises as the psychiatrist—under the guise of medicine—attempts to change values and beliefs. That is not medicine. The pastor is disturbed at having residents from the adjoining lots digging up his backyard to plant corn and tomatoes. He does not object to—but rather encourages—all such activity in the yards next door.

So, in effect, the issue boils down to this: the Bible is the textbook for living before God and neighbor, and the pastor has been ordained to teach and guide God's flock by it. When others take over the work and substitute other textbooks, conflict is inevitable. The most recent change occurred because the pastor took a fresh look at his title deed and resurveyed the land. In the process, he discovered an incredible amount of usurpation by others. He dare not abandon the tract to which God in the Scriptures has given him a clear title. The idea is not to destroy psychology or psychiatry; pastors simply want psychologists and psychiatrists to cultivate their own property.

In all of this, the sovereignty of God has played a conspicuous role. So often, however, when thinking of His sovereignty, we restrict our concerns to the matter of the relation of regeneration to faith. But it is not only in regeneration that God is sovereign; He is sovereign in sanctification as well. If, in order to accomplish His purposes in the believer, He has given His Word to be ministered by His church in the power of His Spirit, that is how these purposes must be accomplished; there can be no other way. And pastors, as key persons in all of this, must see to it that this is the way that things are done—whether it pleases others or not. The ministry of the Word to believers in counseling can be dispensed with no more readily than the ministry of the Word in preaching.

In conclusion, therefore, I wish to emphasize the fact that Nouthetic counseling has issued from a tight theological commitment. The position that has been developed and articulated is the direct result of Reformed thinking. Those who hold to other theological commitments, it might be noted, have viewed the problems in the field quite differently. Because of their failure to acknowledge the sovereignty of God at other points, they cannot hold the line against the defection of autonomous thought and action in counseling either. So, if there is anything that has been done over the last decade that is worthy of mention, it is but the natural outcome of the faithful efforts of those who labored before. For it was they who, against unthinkable odds, held tenaciously to, and in clarity and with power delineated, the scriptural truth of the sovereignty of God in all things. We are now making every effort to apply the principles that they taught us to the task of Christian counseling.

We call upon you—whoever you are, and in whatever way you can—to join with us in this work. It has just begun. During the next ten years, far more can be accomplished if you do. The needs are great, the opportunities are numerous, but the human resources are few. We would stagger at the enormity of the undertaking but for one fact. It is a fact that brings hope and confidence, a fact that is the source of all humility and gratitude.

It is the fact that God is *Sovereign*.

A Certain Inheritance[1]

Paul calls the Spirit, whom [believers] receive, both "Spirit of adoption" and the "seal" and "guarantee of the inheritance to come." For he surely establishes and seals in their hearts by his testimony the assurance of the adoption to come.[2]

—John Calvin

Throughout his writings, John Calvin sounded the note of certainty, and that certainty had a powerful influence on the Reformation. He was especially concerned that believers should know the certainty of their salvation. The Roman Catholic Church's ceremonialism and system of merit had utterly obscured the biblical truth that people can know in this life that they will spend eternity in the presence of God. As a result, many believed that those once saved could be lost again. Calvin wanted to remove the fear that salvation can be lost. Rather, he wanted believers to know that their salvation is assured in Christ, resulting in confidence and love in place of fear.

The scriptural doctrine of the perseverance of the saints, which Calvin strongly championed, was the key to maintaining certainty of salvation. I am delighted to reexamine the biblical evidence for the cheerful and soul-warming teaching of the perseverance of the saints, especially at the present time, when in some "evangelical" circles all of the doctrines established at the Reformation are considered up for grabs.

---

1   This essay is from Burk Parsons, ed., *John Calvin: A Heart for Devotion, Doctrine, and Doxology* (Lake Mary, FL: Reformation Trust Publishing, 2008).
2   John Calvin, *Institutes of the Christian Religion*, ed. John T. McNeill; trans. Ford Lewis Battles; Library of Christian Classics, XX–XXI (Philadelphia: Westminster John Knox, 1960), 3.24.1.

NOTHING CAN GO WRONG WITH OUR INHERITANCE

The clearest statement of the doctrine of perseverance is found in 1 Peter 1:3-5:

> *Blessed be the God and Father of our Lord Jesus Christ! According to his great mercy, he has caused us to be born again to a living hope through the resurrection of Jesus Christ from the dead, to an inheritance that is imperishable, undefiled, and unfading, kept in heaven for you, who by God's power are being guarded through faith for a salvation ready to be revealed in the last time.*

Peter makes it clear that the heavenly inheritance of the saints is secure. There is nothing that can destroy or even mar it, because it is "imperishable, undefiled, and unfading." Earthly things, as Jesus pointed out, have the very opposite characteristics: "moth and rust destroy" them (Matt. 6:19). But the heavenly inheritance is of such a nature that it cannot be so affected. Being a spiritual inheritance, in God's spiritual realm, it is entirely out of the reach of such things.

Calvin writes: "In this way we are assured of the inheritance of the Heavenly Kingdom; for the only Son of God, to whom it wholly belongs, has adopted us as his brothers. 'For if brothers, then also fellow heirs with him' [Rom. 8:17]."[3] So there is no doubt about the integrity of the inheritance—the salvation that Jesus purchased for His own.

Moreover, this inheritance, as Peter says, is "kept in heaven." It is a trust that God has committed into His own hands for safekeeping. If the almighty preserving power of God is being exerted to protect it, then we can be absolutely certain that nothing can go wrong with our future inheritance.

NOTHING CAN GO WRONG WITH THE HEIR

But those who believe that people once saved may lose their salvation often point to the vulnerability of the believer himself. The believer, they think, is the weak link in the chain. "Of course," they say, "no one can

---

3   Ibid., 2.12.2.

snatch him from God's hand, but he can wander and fall from grace on his own." But Peter will have nothing to do with this notion. He knows of no weak link; his words make it perfectly clear that God has covered all the bases. He assures his readers that just as nothing can go wrong with the inheritance, so nothing can go wrong with the heir. He, too, is "guarded by God's power," and there is no power greater than God's—least of all the power of a believer to tear himself loose from God's safekeeping.

Moreover, as some might fail to notice, Peter makes it absolutely plain that the guarding takes place "through faith." That can mean nothing else than that the faith that saves (a gift from God, according to Eph. 2:8-9) is so nurtured and cared for by the Spirit of God that no genuine believer ever apostatizes. The phrase "through faith" is telling for the argument, since it is a supposed loss of faith that is the thrust of the attack by those who believe in the possibility of losing salvation. It is here that they believe the weak link is to be found. But Peter parries their thrust by saying that it is precisely through—by means of—faith that God preserves His people. God's safekeeping "power" works through the faith of the believer. In other words, it is precisely because the power of God is manifested in preserving the Christian's faith that he can be assured of never losing his salvation.

In describing Christ's work as the Mediator of our salvation, Calvin explains how we are heirs according to God's pledge:

> [The Mediator's] task was to restore us to God's grace as to make of the children of men, children of God; of the heirs of Gehenna, heirs of the Heavenly Kingdom. Who could have done this had not the self-same Son of God become the Son of man, and had not so taken what was ours as to impart what was his to us, and to make what was his by nature ours by grace? Therefore, relying on this pledge, we trust that we are sons of God.[4]

The perseverance of believers in the faith is also clearly taught in John 17, a powerful passage that is often misinterpreted. Here we are privileged to listen in on what has been called the High Priestly Prayer of Christ. In

---

4   Ibid.

it, He speaks of believers becoming "one" so that "the world may believe that you have sent me" (v. 21). This prayer has been consistently understood by liberals (and, sadly, of late by conservatives, as well) as teaching that organic union (or, at least, corporate expressions of unity) among Christians will lead the world to believe in Christ. If that were true, then Jesus' prayer has never been answered in the affirmative. Indeed, it could only be declared an utter failure. From the beginning, there have been strife and division among Christians, as the New Testament itself and church history so plainly testify. But, of course, we must maintain that Christ's prayer for unity has not failed. How, then, do we explain the failure of churches to unite? The fact is that He prayed for nothing of the sort.

For what then did Jesus pray? Surely He asked the Father that His followers might become one, didn't He? Yes, He did. But the unity for which He prayed was not a horizontal unity among men; rather, He prayed for a vertical unity with Himself, as He is one with the Father. Many have failed to understand this truth. The entire prayer is a petition that genuine believers may not be "lost" as Judas was (v. 12). Since Christ was about to leave His own, He prayed that God would continue to "guard" them, just as He previously had "kept" them under His watchful care (v. 12). And He prayed not only for the apostles, but also for those who would come to believe under their preaching (v. 20). The kind of guarding that Jesus had in mind is explained in verse 21: "that they may all be one, just as you, Father, are in me, and I in you, that they also may be in us, so that the world may believe that you have sent me."

AN INSEPARABLE UNITY

The unity involved in these words is a unity with the Father and the Son, a unity that is as inseparable as that which these members of the Trinity enjoy. And in answer to His Son's prayer, the Father continues to bring disciples into such union with Jesus and Himself, so that they are "guarded" from anything that might destroy them (vv. 12, 20-21). The world believed when, in the face of great persecution, true Christians refused to abandon their faith. The world could not fail to see that there was something different about them. Many came over to the faith when they saw that neither flame nor rack nor wild beasts could separate them from their love for God and His love for them (Rom. 8:35-39). They recognized that something beyond mere human grit filled the hearts of the martyrs who endured to the end. That something was the Father's answer to Jesus' prayer.

Nothing could be simpler. God doesn't make a promise, then change His mind. He never hands us something with one hand, only to take it back with the other. He would never give eternal life to a person and then later kill him spiritually. Eternal life is just that—life that lasts eternally in God's presence. God is true to His word. The certainty that Calvin taught was nothing new; it was first taught by Jesus, and then by Peter and Paul.

Add one more proof from Romans—the chain of certainty found in Romans 8:30: "And those whom he predestined he also called, and those whom he called he also justified, and those whom he justified he also glorified." There is no weak link in the chain. It moves inexorably from predestination to glorification. The several declarations given by Paul are tied together in such a way that they are not subject to interruptions or alterations. Calvin writes:

> "Those whom he appointed beforehand, he also called; those whom he called, he also justified" [Rom. 8:30] that he might sometime glorify them. Although in choosing his own Lord already has adopted them as his children, we see that they do not come into possession of so great a good except when they are called; conversely, that when they are called, they already enjoy some share of their election. For this reason, Paul calls the Spirit, whom they receive, both "Spirit of adoption" [Rom. 8:15] and the "seal" and "guarantee of the inheritance to come" [Eph. 1:13-14; cf. 2 Cor. 1:22; 5:5]. For he surely establishes and seals in their hearts by his testimony the assurance of the adoption to come.[5]

WHAT ABOUT APOSTASY?

When, for instance, preachers from the heretical denomination called the Churches of Christ[6] speak of "the possibility of apostasy," they mean

---

5   Ibid., 3.24.1.
6   This is an Arminian group, founded by Thomas and Alexander Campbell, that claims to be the only true church. Campbellites refuse to capitalize the word *church*

that those who are truly saved may leave the faith, lose their salvation, and turn against the Lord Jesus Christ. Plainly, the Bible speaks about apostasy, but that is not what it means by the word. A very important verse that makes the truth about apostasy clear is 1 John 2:19: "They went out from us, but they were not of us; for if they had been of us, they would have continued with us. But they went out, that it might become plain that they all are not of us."

In this verse, John is addressing the fact that certain gnostic teachers who had been in the fold had left and had begun teaching their heresy. Previously, they had seemed to be true Christians, because they gave no outward indication of their heretical belief. But their false views of the nature of Christ solidified and came to the fore, and they found that they could no longer fellowship with genuine Christians. So they apostatized and denied that Christ died for our sins.[7]

In this verse, two important facts emerge. First, those who apostatized were never true believers. John says that by leaving, they made it clear that this was so ("they were not of us"). While they had been a part of the visible church, they had never belonged to the invisible church. Their profession of faith was false. This problem of a false profession of faith in Jesus Christ, which we so often encounter in our churches today, was a problem in apostolic times and in the sixteenth century as well. In fact, Calvin describes it as a "daily" occurrence:

> Yet it daily happens that those who seemed to be Christ's, fall away from him again, and hasten to destruction. Indeed, in that same passage, where he declares that none of those whom the Father had given to him perished, he nevertheless excepts the son of perdition [John 17:12]. True indeed, but it is also equally plain that such persons never cleaved to Christ with the heartfelt trust in which certainty of election has, I say, been established for us.[8]

Those who teach that believers may apostatize from the church disregard John's plain explanation of the facts. We must not do so. Instead, we must maintain that those who denounce the faith never had true

---

and claim not to be a denomination.
7 The verb *apostatize* means "to stand off from."
8 Calvin, *Institutes of the Christian Religion*, 3.24.7.

faith in the first place. They may have been among believers, but they were not of them. Otherwise, as John says, they would not have failed to persevere with them.

Second, note the corollary: John affirms that "if they had been of us, they would have continued with us." True believers remain in the faith and in the church. They endure to the end. It is certainly possible for a believer to defect for a time, but, like Peter or John Mark—who both had temporary lapses—in the end they repent and return.

THE AUTHOR OF HEBREWS AGREES

The letter to the Hebrews addresses this problem in strong language in two places (Heb. 6:4-9; 10:26-29). Throughout the book, the writer shows a concern that his readers might "drift" from the truth in the face of persecution (Heb. 2:1; 12:3). This concern about those who might "fall away" leads him to warn of the fearful eventualities that will come to those who do. As a result, the book is replete with both warnings and encouragements.

While he knew that true believers would not repudiate their Savior, the writer recognized the possibility that some among his readers might not be genuine Christians after all. Therefore, he shows that people may become a part of the visible body of Christ, participating in all of God's wonderful benefits that are provided for the life of the church, but eventually turn their backs on everything they have experienced. There is no way to renew such people to a genuine profession of faith, he says, because there is only one true message—the very one they have rejected. So he describes how great a dishonor to Christ it is for one to hear and taste the gospel only to reject it, and how terrible are the consequences.

But as he describes the situation in terms of an example, he seems to conclude that his readers' faith is genuine—at least the faith of most of those to whom he is writing. The example is that of the rain watering the ground. The very same rain (teaching, Christian fellowship, etc.) falls on two patches of ground. One produces fruit, while the other produces thorns and thistles. The first result refers to those who believe and persevere; the latter refers to those who do not.

Then, applying that example to his readers, he declares: "In your case, beloved, we feel sure of better things—things that belong to salvation."

Here the writer says that those who have salvation do not fall away. They do not apostatize.

GOD IS A GOOD FATHER

To teach that a saved person may be lost is to impugn the fatherhood of God. It is to say that He so poorly raises His children that many become delinquents who "drop out" or must be disowned by Him. But the Bible teaches otherwise. Hebrews says that the Lord "disciplines" each of His children in order to bring them into line when they go the wrong way; if they receive no discipline, the book teaches, they are illegitimate (Heb. 12:5-11). Such discipline, we are assured, "yields the peaceful fruit of righteousness to those who have been trained by it" (v. 11). God disciplines all of His legitimate children, and His discipline gets positive results.[9] God does not allow rebellious children to wander away from the family or become so incorrigible that He must put them out. Those members who leave, or who are permanently put out of the church, as we have seen, are false professors. Calvin writes:

> In order that we may quickly summarize the whole matter, let this stand as the first of two distinctions: wherever punishment is for vengeance, there the curse and wrath of God manifest themselves, and these he always withholds from believers. On the other hand, chastisement is a blessing of God and also bears witness to his love, as Scripture teaches [Job 5:17; Prov. 3:11-12; Heb. 12:5-6].[10]

This is by no means a merely academic discussion. To believe that one can be saved and lost leads to several serious consequences. For instance, a young man who had been taught this unbiblical doctrine once told me that he had finally "given up." Since, as he had discovered, he could not "keep himself saved," but supposedly kept falling in and out of salvation, he had concluded that he might as well live it up for whatever pleasures he could enjoy here and now in this life. After all, he would never reach heaven. According to all indications, he was not using this description and explanation of his experience as an excuse.

---

9 Cf. Rev. 3:19.
10 Calvin, *Institutes of the Christian Religion*, 3.4.32.

PERSEVERANCE IS THE KEY

If you have been taught the "once saved, always saved" doctrine, you may think that there is no difference between that teaching and the doctrine of the perseverance of the saints. But while it is certainly true that those who are once saved will always be saved, the concept of the perseverance of the saints encompasses a vitally important truth that is rarely emphasized by people who teach the "once saved, always saved" view. That missing emphasis is the fact that a person is saved *through* perseverance, not apart from it. The "once saved, always saved" view may lead those who hold it into quietistic thinking. That is to say, they may think that they have little or no part to play in maintaining their salvation, but that God does it all for them. While a person is not saved by works (as Romanists believe) and does not remain saved because of works (as the Churches of Christ believe), God saves only those who persevere in the faith.

In a section of the *Institutes of the Christian Religion* titled "Perseverance is exclusively God's work; it is neither a reward nor a complement of our individual act," Calvin writes:

> Perseverance would, without any doubt, be accounted God's free gift if a most wicked error did not prevail that it is distributed according to men's merit, in so far as each man shows himself receptive to the first grace. But since this error arose from the fact that men thought it in their power to spurn or to accept the proffered grace of God, when the latter opinion is swept away the former idea also falls of itself. However, there is a twofold error here. For besides teaching that our gratefulness for the first grace and our lawful use of it are rewarded by subsequent gifts, they add also that grace does not work in us by itself, but is only a co-worker with us.[11]

Perseverance is the result of the work of the Spirit in believers' hearts. Nevertheless, it is a work that enables them to keep on believing, as Peter says. God does not believe for them. Rather, they are "guarded" through faith.

---

11 Ibid., 2.3.11.

In John 15, we read about the sanctification that is necessary for a believer to be saved.[12] A so-called "abiding" condition, which some Higher Life adherents take to mean a special sort of holiness, is not taught in the passage. That idea distorts the apostle's teaching. The Greek word *meno*, which the King James Version translates as "abide," means "remain, continue, stay." It does not refer to some special state of "resting" in Christ that only super saints achieve. Rather, this abiding is equivalent to persevering in the faith. And it is true not of a select few, such as the apostles only, but of all Christians. Indeed, persevering in one's faith in Christ is necessary not only for bearing "much fruit," as the passage teaches, but also for salvation.

Unless one remains in the vine, "he is thrown away like a branch and withers," eventually to be burned up (v. 6). Jesus, therefore, commands, "Abide [or remain] in my love" (v. 9b). The apostles had to persevere in their faith or be cast aside like a branch broken off the vine, and the same is true for all believers. Christ, the Vine, requires every professed Christian to remain in Him by genuine faith or eventually be thrown into the fire.

So perseverance is the result of true faith, nourished and maintained by the Spirit. But the believer himself must continue to exercise it. He may never sit back and say, "I'm saved, I may do as I please, since I can never be lost." To think that way indicates either that he has received very faulty teaching or that he is not a believer. No one who is truly converted can think that way for very long, if at all. True Spirit-given and Spirit-nourished faith leads to biblical thinking. A professed Christian must persevere—remain, continue, stay—in the Vine.

Jesus spoke not only of believers remaining in Him, but also of His "words" remaining in believers (v. 7). Moreover, in verse 14 He said, "You are my friends if you do what I command you." After justification, by means of divinely guarded faith, one remains in salvation by the work of the Spirit, who, through that faith, enables him to continue obeying Jesus' words and commandments. That is perseverance.

---

12   I.e., the sanctification that is always present, giving evidence of the fact that one is saved.

This precious doctrine of the perseverance of the saints, coming down to us from the Reformation, must be preserved at all costs. We may neither abandon it nor compromise with those who would do so. The certainty of salvation, which Calvin so dearly wished his congregation to know and which he bequeathed to subsequent generations, must not be lost.

Counseling and the Five Points of Calvinism[1]

As recently as 15 years ago, eyebrows would rise everywhere (even in Reformed circles) at the announcement of the topic assigned to me: "The Bible in Counseling." That is no longer true. During a period when liberalism had gained ascendancy and in which the conservative church was ill-prepared to do battle on all fronts, the practical side of her ministry was neglected. This virtually led to an abandonment of the ministry of counseling, to which (in a theologically naive and unsystematic, but nevertheless consistent, manner) she had addressed herself since the days of the apostles. In fighting for the Bible, which was the very basis of her life, the church lost sight of some of those purposes for which the Bible had been given.[2]

Consequently, there appeared alternatives to fill the vacuum: views of unconverted theorists like Freud, Adler, Skinner, Rogers, *et.al.* began to gain authority inside the church herself. And sadly, the church, even the evangelical, Reformed church, was willing to have it so. She bought into these views, and in short order, eclecticism in counseling (that is, the counseling that was farmed out to "professionals" who espoused similar views) became the name of the game.

Prior to this, indeed from biblical days, counseling, along with preaching, had been considered an essential part of the ministry of the Word (cf. Col. 1:28; Acts 20:31, etc.). As such, there was no problem in using the Bible as the textbook for this work of counseling. But when

---
1 This essay was originally presented as an address entitled "The Bible in Counseling," delivered at the National Presbyterian and Reformed Fellowship Congress in Grand Rapids, Michigan. It was published in booklet form in 1981.
2 E.g., II Tim. 3: I 5-17. Here, the Bible, we are plainly told, was given (1) to lead men to salvation (evangelism) and (2) to change saved men (edification), (3) through ministry (ecclesiology).

eclectic thought not only gained a foothold, but at length became firmly entrenched and institutionalized in Bible-believing strongholds, counseling and preaching were unceremoniously pried apart and came to be considered two distinct activities, having no integral relationship to one another. Pastors continued to base preaching upon the Bible, to which they (more or less) turned for its warrant, its content, and its method, while increasingly, counseling was thought to do with an area of life to which the Scriptures do not address themselves. This double divorce between counseling and the Scriptures, and counseling and preaching explains the lifted eyebrows.

I am truly thankful, therefore, for the change in Reformed circles today that not only allows us to relax our eyebrows but also led the planning committee of the National Presbyterian and Reformed Fellowship (NPRF) to determine to consider this topic under the theme "The Word of the Sovereign God." I am delighted that there are those in the NPRF who believe that the Bible ought to be used in counseling. Once again, Reformed Christians everywhere are learning how to minister the liberating Truth of the living God to persons caught up in the miseries of a world under a curse!

Moreover, I am grateful not only for my topic, but for the overall theme of this conference. Taking my lead from the two seems to be the wisest way for me to chart and direct the course I shall follow in this paper. Let us, then, consider what we are doing here today. In the wording of the topic and theme, I see at least three main facts that might be emphasized:
1. God is sovereign.
2. That sovereign God has given us His Word, the Bible, in which He tells us that
3. He wants us to use that Word in counseling.

Since the NPRF doesn't seem to doubt these fundamental principles, and by assigning this topic under this theme asserts as much, I need not discuss them at length. It is, perhaps, enough to suggest (but not to consider) that the third point—God wants us to use His Word in counseling—might be subdivided into the following statements:
- The Bible provides the *warrant* for Christian counseling.
- The Bible provides the *authority* for Christian counseling.

- The Bible provides the *content* for Christian counseling.
- The Bible provides the *principles* for Christian counseling.

Rather than retrace old material,[3] after a few preliminary comments, I would like to turn to fresher considerations. There is still much uncharted territory in the field of biblical counseling. But first, let me orient you just a bit.

I don't want to spend too much time discussing the general theme of the conference because, doubtless, others will also have much to say about God's sovereignty. Yet it is important to observe at least one or two of the implications for counseling that grow out of the fact of God's sovereignty.[4]

It is plain that a sovereign God, who has made human beings, has the right to tell them how to live, how not to live, and what to do about their lives if and when they fail to live as He has commanded. In both preaching and counseling, therefore, the ministry of the Word concerns itself with such questions. Both have to do with leading people to love God and their neighbors. Thus, we minister the Scriptures not only to make people "wise about salvation" (II Tim. 3:15), but also because they are "useful for teaching, for conviction, for correction and for disciplined training in righteousness" (II Tim. 3:16).[5]

We shall return to this theme presently. For now, it is sufficient to observe that the sovereign God Himself teaches in the Scriptures that they were given for the very purpose for which counseling exists: to effect definitive, lasting change that pleases God (II Tim. 3:16 sets forth such a process of change).[6]

Written just as clearly on the other side of the page (of course) is the obligation of God's creatures to obey His sovereign commandments. If the Scriptures teach us what He commands, point out to us where we fail to measure up to those commandments, show us how to get out of the misery into which we plunge ourselves when we fail, and train us

---

[3] All of these issues have been discussed in my books at length.
[4] I have developed others in my chapter *Counseling and the Sovereignty of God*.
[5] All Bible quotations are from my translation in the *Christian Counselor's New Testament and Proverbs*.
[6] For a thorough explanation of this process see my book *How to Help People Change*.

in alternate lifestyles that help us to please God and stay out of sinful pathways, then we are obligated as well to learn what the Scriptures say about such matters, and (by God's Spirit) to observe them prayerfully. And, since it is the Scriptures that effect such change, counselors are obligated to use the Scriptures in their ministry to counselees.

The redeemed body of believers (together with their children) that we call the church is under a double obligation to obey, since it consists of persons who stand in a unique relationship to the sovereign God. They are not only His creatures, and therefore subject to His lordship, but they also are members of His family and must obey His parental will. As the risen Lord (moreover), Jesus Christ is the Head and King of the church.

That double-barrelled fact—God has a right to command (as sovereign Creator and sovereign Father over His people) and we have an obligation to obey (as creatures, subjects, and children)—is true not only in general but specifically in relationship to the church's ministry of counseling. She must counsel for the reasons He requires, to achieve the ends and purposes He has in view according to the ways that He has designated—in the Bible. If the sovereign God commands, we must do what He commands. We are not free to set up our own purposes and principles for counseling; we have no warrant to adopt methods neither sanctioned by nor consistent with those principles of counseling that He has set forth in the Scriptures. In short, if God has given the Bible to "equip us fully" for the work of changing people's lives, then we need not, indeed, we dare not, turn elsewhere to discover how to counsel. Like Jesus Christ, the perfect Counselor, we too can find all we really need for a faithful ministry of counseling in the Scriptures.

Let me go further and say this: If the sovereign God has commanded His church to counsel (as a part of the ministry of the Word) and has provided all that is necessary for the pursuit of this task (in the Scriptures), it is rebellion (out of ignorance or not) for the church to turn to other sources. If, as I have shown elsewhere,[7] there is biblical warrant for counseling, biblical content to inform counseling and biblical principles

---

[7] I do not wish to cite specific references or develop this theme further here, since (in one way or another) I have dealt with this question in a number of books.

in accordance with which counseling may (and ought to) be carried out (and from which a system of biblical counseling may be constructed), then any other system must be viewed as competitive, not only to the church and her ministry, but (of greater importance) to God and God's Word.[8] It is a serious affront to the sovereign God, therefore, when Freud, Rogers, Skinner, or any other theorist sets up his own system claiming to accomplish, without the Bible, precisely what God designed the Bible itself to do. The Spirit's fruit is produced only by the Spirit, blessing His Word.

Even more to the point, it is a sin for a Christian minister (not to speak of a Reformed pastor who acknowledges God's sovereignty in Scripture) to defend such competitive systems, to use precepts and practices from these systems in counseling, and (as so often is done) to palm off these views and approaches as "Christian" or "biblical."[9] Countering that problem, to put it simply, has been one of my concerns for many years.

However, that is not my main concern in this essay, as, indeed, it has not been my major interest in any of my books. I have torn down (I freely admit), but I have worked ten times as hard at building up.[10] I have tried—with whatever success (you may judge; I won't)—to replace every false approach with a biblical one. As a result, a system of truly Christian counseling, based on biblical exegesis and theological reflection, has been developed. Since it is now well known,[11] I shall take no time to describe that system here. Rather, I wish to devote the larger portion of this essay to what I consider to be a very important but totally neglected area: counseling and the five points of Calvinism. I have chosen this track because of the emphasis in this congress upon God's sovereignty.

But first, please allow me one more brief excursus. I do want to note that intensive work in biblical counseling has only begun. There lies before us so much to do that it staggers me to think about it. I am encouraged to think that a number of other men have begun to undertake some

---
8   Cf. the introduction and chapter one of my book *Theology of Counseling* for detailed discussion of this point.
9   See especially *Your Place in the Counseling Revolution*.
10   See my discussion of this in *What About Nouthetic Counseling?*
11   Though often known only by misrepresentation and gossip, and, therefore, not truly known.

of the tasks that must be pursued. But by comparison to the enormous amount of work that remains virtually untouched, what they can do will make only a dent in it. Scholarly pastors, everywhere, who have been engaged in the practice of Christian counseling must become involved. Not only must they continue to counsel (and to teach their elders and deacons how to counsel), but they must contribute the exegetical and practical insights that they have gained to help the rest of us. The task cannot be done by only a few.

I am happy, therefore, to be able to issue a call to Reformed counselors, urging them to join us in the work. There is no group better prepared and equipped to do so. Reformed pastors ought to be taking the leadership in the field; after all, they have the theology, the training, and the tools, and it is they who understand what the command of a sovereign God means.

Why, then, are they so slack? Can it be that in asserting God's sovereignty, they have stressed His decretive will and forgotten His directive will? Have they focused on God's eternal decree to the neglect of His requirements in His Word? Has human responsibility been set aside? Surely, if that is so, if an impractical, abstract theological statement of biblical truth is what we all too often have settled for, then this conference, with its accent upon The Word of the Sovereign God, is designed to summon us back to a better balance.

It is a matter of balance, of course. There is no conflict between the two: God has ordained all things that come to pass. But that same God has also sovereignly ordained that He will work out His purposes not only directly (as in creation and miracles), but through human agency. Let me, therefore, be one to underscore and applaud the theme with all its implications for practical living and ministry.

Now, to the five points of Calvinism. Actually, as you know, they are the five Calvinistic responses to points of Arminian attack upon Reformation teaching.) How frequently Reformed people (and even Reformed pastors) have failed to appreciate the practical implications of their faith! In a brief, suggestive (but non-definitive) way, therefore, I would like to pursue a slim few of the counseling implications of the five points of Calvinism. I shall not attempt to prove the biblical nature of these five points; in a gathering of the NPRF that can (and will) be presupposed.

Total Depravity

Reformed counselors, from the outset, ought to have been crystal clear about the fact that it is impossible to bring about deep change in unbelievers through counseling. Yet, all too often, many counselors, led astray by eclectic influences rather than following the implications of biblical doctrine, have attempted to do just that. All persons, descended from Adam by natural generation, are born not only guilty because of the representative character of Adam's sin, but corrupt (and miserable) as a consequence of it. This corruption and misery, as the heading indicates, is total. It is pervasive. Every part of man—his intellectual, volitional, and emotional capacities—is affected. No part of man has escaped the blighting impact of the fall. Its effects are total. However, that does not mean that in any aspect (even though every aspect is corrupt), man is as depraved as he might be. God's common grace has restrained human wickedness so that this totality within the totality does not occur.

Yet it truly may be said, "Man is dead in trespasses and sin." A dead person cannot be induced by human effort to make the sort of changes in his life that God requires and that he so desperately needs. Another human being, no matter how good a counselor (or even how biblical) he may be, has no power to bring about the needed changes. This spiritual death constitutes nothing less than utter separation from God. The unregenerate person is dead to God, to the Bible, and to the sanctifying work of the Holy Spirit; he is (in short) dead to biblical change. And counseling will not change that fact.

Since this is so, Reformed counselors should be the first to recognize that it is useless to try to counsel unbelievers. Since man's basic problem is spiritual death, nothing short of spiritual life will do (cf. Rom. 8:8). Depraved persons can change, of course, but when they do so, they merely exchange one wrong practice or pattern for another. The change is external and superficial. Much counseling amounts to little more than assisting them in such fruitless endeavors. But to do so in God's Name—as if futility, in exchange for futility, were all that Christian counseling had to offer—is totally unacceptable. Christ has not called us to a ministry of reformation; He has something better to offer: transformation. And we dare not misrepresent God. To do so is to dishonor Him and to mislead non-Christians.

The consequence of this truth is that unbelievers cannot be counseled biblically. Instead, they must be precounseled (or to use the more familiar term) evangelized.[12] Reformed counseling, therefore, must provide a place for evangelism. Any system that makes no such provision clearly cannot be biblical (or Reformed). The doctrine of total depravity, then, implies that there is a need for total transformation, change in the whole man at a level of depth (where "all things become new")—a change of the heart that occurs only in regeneration.

Unconditional Election

God has chosen some to be saved; in the Bible He calls them "the elect" (or, as the word means, "select") to indicate this choice. The choice was unconditional; i.e., God freely chose those He wished to save, not on the basis of any virtue, merit, worth, foreseen faith, or any other factor in them. The choice was made entirely within God, out of His own good pleasure. This selection of some for eternal life was made on the basis of unrevealed factors known to God alone. Since they are unrevealed, we must not speculate about why God chose to set His saving love on one person and not on another (cf. Deut. 29:29).

But one thing is clear: even though we do not know why particular individuals were chosen over others, God has revealed something of His general purpose in choosing the elect. He wishes:

1. To honor Himself by making His mercy known in their redemption (Romans 9:23).
2. To constitute His church as a holy and blameless people to stand before him (Ephesians 1:4).

These stated purposes should encourage the Christian counselor and generate hope for his counseling of believers. All that is untrue of the unregenerate happily is true of regenerate counselees. Since God determined to choose some to become a holy people, and since He has sent the "Spirit of holiness" (i.e., the Spirit who produces holiness) into them to make them holy, there is every reason to counsel with confidence and

---

12 I have discussed evangelism in counseling more fully in another essay in this book.

expectation. Change at a level of depth is always possible when counseling the members of God's flock.

Reformed counselors know that holiness ultimately depends upon God's electing decree and not upon the counselor himself (yet that does not negate or lessen the responsibility of either the counselor or the counselee; God has determined to bring about His will through—not apart from—responsible human action). Because of this knowledge that God has elected and saved some who will grow in holiness, Reformed counselors may counsel with an assurance and hope that others do not possess. God has promised to use the ministry of His Word to effect holiness (sanctification), and even though Christians may neglect or reject that Word for a time, the Reformed counselor knows that in time, God will have His way. He is sovereign; those whom He has chosen to be a holy people will (progressively in this life and completely in the life to come) be made holy. It is a hope often realized, then, that through Christian counseling sessions, God will work. It is exciting to begin counseling with such expectations. There is always the possibility that "today, in this session," God will use the ministry of His Word to break into a human life and transform it.

Moreover, even in the exercise of human agency by the counselor and counselee, it is comforting for the Reformed counselor to know that change does not depend upon unaided human action. It is the Spirit who prompts both counselor and counselee to read the Word, and who enables them to understand it. It is also the Spirit who encourages them to obey it and who strengthens them in doing so (Phil. 2:13; Gal. 3:3ff.). To know that one is involved in the ministry of God's Word by which God accomplishes sanctification in elect persons is not only an exciting but also an immensely satisfying experience.

It is at this point, perhaps, that a note of caution must be sounded. No other person (as a private individual) may judge that another is elect or deny that he is. God alone infallibly knows this fact (I Sam. 16:7). The counselee is urged to make his "calling and election sure" to himself (II Pet. 1:10). He can have strong assurance of the fact. But others can judge only outer actions and words; they may not judge his heart. Counselors have been given no mandate to judge the hearts of counselees.

Nevertheless, there are two ways in which one may make a functional (not absolute) judgment about another's salvation:
1. if he should leave the church of Christ as an apostate (I John 2:19);
2. if he is excommunicated for contumacy (Matt. 18:17b).

But please note, such judgments are functional only. That is, they tell one how to relate to another at a given time; they do not constitute absolute judgment about the state of his soul before God. Persons outside of the church may be believers (in rebellion, wrongly disciplined by the church, etc.) who, in time, will repent or, in one way or another, find their way back into the fellowship of the body. But while separated, they must be treated as unbelievers. That is to say, the church must relate to them as to non-Christians.

All of this discussion leads to the conclusion that it is possible for the counselor to find himself counseling a professing member of an evangelical (and even Reformed) church who may not be truly regenerate. In such cases, since it is impossible to know his or her heart, the counselor treats the counselee *as regenerate* on the basis of his profession of faith. But note that counseling (if it is truly Christian in objectives and orientation) *will fail*. An unregenerate person cannot, and will not, make *biblical* changes. The failure will focus ultimately upon either (1) an unwillingness to submit to Christ in His Word or (2) an inability to do so (or both). In some cases, the counseling itself will lead to a recognition of a false profession of faith and/or the need for church discipline (evangelism, of course, may be effective). But a member of an evangelical church should (in love) be presumed to be a Christian until his actions or words prove otherwise (cf. I Cor. 13:7). The functional "proof" I have in mind is the ultimate unwillingness to submit to Christ's authority, rightly exercised by the church (Matt. 13:15ff.).

Limited Atonement

Because everyone limits the atonement (the Calvinist limits its scope; the Arminian limits its effectiveness), it is not only Calvinists who should be called upon to explain their point of view. Arminians have some explaining to do, too. But that is beside the point at present.

This wonderful, warm biblical doctrine means that Jesus Christ is truly a *personal* Savior. Many people rightly affirm that truth who have no idea why He is. Christ didn't die impersonally for "mankind" as a whole. "Mankind" is a cold, nonexistent abstraction. Instead, He died for particular persons for whose particular sins He suffered and rendered complete satisfaction to God by bearing their punishment. Every believer may truly say, "He died for my lies."

What does this mean for counselors? Many things, but consider this: the counselor can assure every true believer that no matter how difficult his circumstances may be, Jesus Christ knows and cares. He has taken a *personal interest* in this counselee and is indeed personally interested in the counseling session going on at the moment. Not only does He know and care about sparrows that fall and number the hairs of one's head, "but," the counselor may observe,

> *If He didn't spare His own Son, but delivered Him up for all of us, won't He also with Him freely give us everything? (Romans 8:32).*

Here, the argument moves from the atonement to God's concern about everyday affairs. It is an argument from the greater to the lesser: God, in His concern to save us, gave His best (Jesus); surely, then, you can expect that out of His great concern, He will meet all lesser needs. And, Paul assures us, this is true for "all of us" (i.e., all of the elect). None can deny this for himself; God's promise is to all of His people.

The personal nature of the atonement demonstrates to us God's personalized interest in each elect child of His. Counseling is not some sort of deistic, impersonal process. God is at work in the ministry of His Word. He is a Father who cares for each individually. This is a truth that many counselees need to hear. Nothing more firmly establishes the fact than the doctrine of limited atonement (or as it is sometimes called, particular redemption).

Irresistible Grace

Few truths could be more encouraging. God calls His elect by an *effectual* call. The Spirit's inner call to life is performative: the call itself brings about the fact (John 5:25). Regeneration does not depend upon some prior preparation by the counselee. He contributes nothing to regeneration. It is not dependent upon the sinner's proper response to the outer call that is extended to all; a proper response is the *result* of the effective power of inner grace. Irresistible grace, producing regeneration, is a sovereign act of Christ through His Spirit by which He quickens (or gives life) to dead sinners (Eph. 2:5). God is active; the dead sinner is wholly passive (as in any concept of a resurrection; cf. again John 5:25). Not only does possession of this new life make all truly biblical counseling possible, but it means that he has a quality of life that opens the possibility of a brand new sort of existence from now on (cf. I Cor. 2).

This "newness of life" (as Paul calls it in Rom. 6) sets us free from sin's dominion. Vicious habits that were acquired previously (in patterns developed as the response of a sinful nature to problems), but that could never be altered, now may be exchanged for new, righteous ones (cf. Rom. 6-8). Peter puts it this way:

> *. . . be deeply concerned about how you behave during your residence as aliens, knowing that you weren't set free from your useless behavior patterns that were passed down from your forefathers, by the payment of a corruptible ransom like silver or gold, but with Christ's valuable blood, shed like the blood of a spotless and unblemished lamb (I Pet. 1:17-19).*

He enlarges on this later in the same letter:

> *As a result [of Christ's death] it is now possible to live the remainder of your time in the flesh no longer following human desires, but following the will of God (I Pet. 4:2).*

This is what God has done for His elect people by regeneration. The quickening (or life-giving) of the Spirit has freed them from slavery to their old ways and has made it possible to walk in altogether new ways. The penalty for sin was paid on the cross; sin's power was broken in regeneration. There is a new heart (disposition of the inner life) in the regenerate person.

Surely, then, biblical counselors may hold out extraordinary expectations of change to their believing counselees. The Reformed counselor need not take the traditional psychoanalytic stance ("This may take a long time, and I can guarantee nothing") but, rather, may assure a regenerate counselee that the God who gave him life from the grave can make great changes in his life--quickly. The Reformed counselor ought not to speak about "patching up marriages" or "getting you back to the place where you used to be." The same Spirit who gave him the new life in the first place can effect changes by counseling that enables the counselee to have a marriage that sings! He can tell him that "God may turn all these liabilities into assets so that (in the end) you may grow far beyond where you were before this difficulty arose. "God is engaged in the work of sanctifying His people whom He has called; counseling (when it is truly the ministry of the Word) is a part of that sanctifying process. The counselor, then, joyfully joins the regenerate counselee in a venture into fuller realization of the life that Christ came to give abundantly. That is his stance.

Perseverance of the Saints

Yes, "once saved, always saved"; that is one way to put it. But whenever we do, it is also important to say that this is not *in spite of* what the believer does but *because* he perseveres. It is true too, that he will thank God for enabling him to persevere; as before, so here, *all is by sovereign grace*.

But, even though the truth of Philippians 2:13 may never be forgotten ("…it is God who is producing in you both the willingness and the ability to do the things that please Him"), the counselor (as do the Scriptures everywhere) must call upon the counselee to persevere to the end. Human responsibility (strengthened by divine help, to be sure) brings about perseverance. The branch must "remain" or "stay" (the King James translation "abide" confuses people) in the vine (John 15). Believers must persevere.

Though they often fall back into their old ways, the elect—every last one of them—will persevere. God Himself says so. According to Peter, nothing can happen to the heir or to his inheritance (I Peter 1:3-5); both are guarded by God's power until the last time. Paul assures us that the gifts and calling of God are not subject to recall (Rom. 11:29). In the same book, he says that God freely grants eternal life as a gift (Rom. 3:23), and speaks of the salvation of Christians as their call (Rom. 1:6). Here, then, is the syllogism of security:

- God's gifts and calling are not recalled;
- God's people receive salvation as a gift and calling.
- Therefore, salvation can never be recalled.

What does this great truth mean to counselors? Does it lead to counselee lethargy? No, quite to the contrary; those who are always concerned about preserving their salvation by their own efforts find their basic orientation inward; they have little time for service to God and ministry to their neighbors. They tend to become introspective. Reformed counselors can help lead counselees into full assurance of their faith, so that they can become useful to God's work. And it is interesting that one makes his calling and election sure (to himself) by depending upon God's promise and then becomes "active" and "fruitful" in developing and using the qualities listed in II Peter 1:5-8, 10.

Moreover, since true Christians will persevere, Reformed counselors ought not to give up on them when at first (or second or third, for that matter) they fail to respond. There is always hope for a regenerate person. All the resources of God are available. True, counseling may take time and effort; there may be disappointments, ups and downs. But through whatever it takes—conviction, reproof, encouragement, urging, church discipline, or whatever else is biblically required—the Christian counselor must have "complete patience" and continue to "teach fully" (II Tim. 4:2). He may stop temporarily, but he must soon begin again to urge his counselee to take whatever scriptural steps he has not been taking (whether because of disobedience or ignorance—hence the reproof, instruction, etc.). In it all, he is to be patient with his counselee. This patience, so essential for all counseling, grows from the biblical conviction that God's saints persevere. Thus, we may never give up on them.

Well, to what point has our brief excursion through biblical teaching about God's sovereignty taken us? I think that we can close with a few concluding statements:

1. Only the sovereign God of Scripture can change people as they ought to be changed. Let us thank Him that He does!
2. The Bible has been given by the Holy Spirit as the instrument that He uses to bring about these changes in regenerate persons.
3. Counselors must use the Bible in counseling so that God's changes may be effected in His way by His power.
4. Because of God's sovereign promises to His elect, and because of His vast resources, Christian counselors ought to counsel with great patience and hope, in joyous anticipation of observing God transform lives dramatically.
5. Counselors must precounsel (or evangelize) unbelievers and not hold out false hope that God will change their lives apart from the gospel.

There is more here, and much that has not been mentioned, but these few suggestive thoughts alone should make the superiority of Christian counseling from a Reformed perspective apparent[13] and should encourage Reformed pastors to engage in such work.

---

13   Many persons who would not call themselves "Reformed," of course do take such a stance toward counseling because it is biblical. I care little for the word "Reformed" (apart from its great historical ties), so long as they wish to be biblical. In my book, it is enough to be biblical—the more biblical one is, the more Reformed he becomes.

Counseling the Unbeliever[1]

THE topic tonight is "How do you counsel an Unbeliever?" What do you do when an unbeliever comes to you for counseling? Now I have held hundreds of conferences with pastors, and I don't believe that I can remember a single conference where there was a question-and-answer period in which someone did not ask the question, in one form or another, "How do you counsel an unbeliever?" So, instead of having that question raised in this conference, I shall address it right now.

You cannot counsel believers and unbelievers the same way

First, let me say that you're going to discover that there will be significant differences between counseling an unbeliever and counseling a believer. If you counsel Christians and unbelievers the same way, there's something wrong with your counseling. You're not doing biblical counseling. Indeed, you've missed the most significant point of all: Does the man know Jesus Christ as his Savior or not? There could be no more significant first question to ask. It may be provisional, to be sure, but at least some kind of answer to this question is necessary as you begin to counsel people. If you don't think that it makes any difference, that tells me your counseling is deficient, and I think that this deficiency will appear as we develop this theme a bit tonight.

Counseling—Christian and non-Christian—has one goal in view: to change people. Everybody who counsels believes that people need to be changed. The hope is to change people's lives. But the first and most significant difference between Christian and non-Christian counseling lies in the kind of change that other systems have in view.

---

1   Adapted from an address given to the second annual conference of the National Association of Nouthetic Counselors (NANC) in 1977.

All non-Christian systems, regardless of what they say, are really changing people on a superficial level. ***All*** unbiblical systems, even when they speak of doing depth counseling, change people at a surface level. No unbiblical method of counseling can really get down into the heart of a human being and change him at that level. But that's exactly what a Christian system must do, to be truly Christian.

In Matthew 15, Jesus talked about man. He said, "From the heart come evil thoughts, murder, adultery, sexual sins, thefts, false testimonies, blasphemies; these are what defile a person, but to eat with unwashed hands doesn't defile a person" (vs. 19). "Out of the heart," says Jesus, "these things come." And this list was not exhaustive, but suggestive of the kinds of things people do that get them into trouble. Then they come for counseling. But what is the source of these problems? The source is the heart: "Out of the heart these things come," Jesus said.

Freud and others who have followed his psychoanalytical approach talk about depth counseling. They speak about getting down into the deepest recesses of a human being, where his motivation really stems from, but they don't have even the faintest idea of what is really involved. Yet, pastors have often been told (and their parishioners have often thought), "Oh now, this man's problem is ***much too deep*** (the key word that is used all the time is "deep") for a pastor to handle. He will need more professional help. I'll have to send him off to a psychiatrist." My friends, it ought to be the other way around! The only person who can really operate at a level of depth is the person who knows how to go to the ***heart*** of a man's problem. That's because the heart ***is*** the man's problem. The only way to go to the heart of a man's problem is through the gospel of Jesus Christ ministered in the power of the Holy Spirit, who transforms the heart of man and ***thus*** transforms his life patterns. The murders, the adulteries, the evil thoughts, the sexual sins, the thefts, the false testimonies, the blasphemies (and all the rest) can be changed only in some superficial way, unless the heart out of which they come and by which they are generated is transformed by the Spirit of God using His Word. And—never forget this—in such work the pastor is the professional—God's professional.

Now we ought to believe that if we believe the Bible. I don't need to turn to twenty-five other passages and do a lot of Bible flipping with you; I don't believe in doing that kind of study (it's not the kind of study to do in the pulpit). You can go home and do that on your own. We only need one verse to tell us something, and we should believe it. But there are at least 125 passages that clearly tell us in one way or another that man's problem stems from sin down deep in the heart with which he was born. He inherited a heart corrupted by Adam's sin. And unless something can get at that corrupt heart, a man really won't be changed at the level of depth that is necessary to alter the source of his problems. Anything else that is done is equivalent to putting a plug in the bottle, putting a lid on the problem, or screwing a cap over it, but it isn't getting to the source that generated the problem. You can't really solve a person's problem at the level of depth necessary unless you use the Word of God, empowered by the Spirit of God, and bring it home to his heart.

The Bible uses a number of terms to talk about human beings. It speaks, for instance, of loving the Lord your God with "all your heart, all your mind, all your soul and all your strength." These words—heart, mind, soul, strength—all describe aspects of the human makeup. It's not quite as easy to cut and categorize people as some think. They make easy divisions like "man is spirit, soul, and body" that don't quite fit the fullness of the scriptural description of man. "Heart" is a word that encompasses all the other inner terms. The term, however, doesn't mean what we mean when we say "heart" today in our society. When somebody says, "I love you with all my heart," he's thinking about one thing—feelings and emotions. The Valentine's Day heart typifies the modern usage. There you see lace doilies, cupids, and cherry-cheeked cherubs with bows and arrows shooting arrows into hearts. Today, "heart" means emotion, feeling. But that isn't what the heart is in the Bible. When you read passages in the Bible that use the word heart, you must never interpret the meaning in terms of the feelings or you will misunderstand every one of those passages. Perhaps some of you have been doing so for years. If so, it's high time you realized it.

When the Bible talks about feelings, it talks not about the *heart* but about the *bowels*—the guts. Did you know that? It does. It speaks about "bowels (feelings) of compassion." The Bible is much closer to the facts than we are in our modern culture. The Bible calls the bowels the seat of the emotions. Where is it that people get ulcers—on the heart? No—in the gut, where so much emotion is centered.

Well then, what does the Bible mean by "heart" if it is not talking about feelings? What the Scriptures are talking about is the inner life of a human being. This is the inner man and his whole inner life, including feelings, thinking, decision-making, etc. "Why do you reason thus in your heart?" asks Jesus. Plans are said to originate in the heart. When a person talks to himself ("the fool has said in his heart …"), he does so in the heart. That is where one thinks with himself, reasons with himself, accuses and excuses himself, etc. According to the Bible, that whole inner life that you live is your heart.

You do know that you live two lives (or one life on two fronts), don't you? You live a life in reference to other people, and you live a life in reference to yourself. And of course, you live both of them in reference to God. God is over both of them. What is it that makes you do what you do? What is it that makes you think what you think? What is it that motivates you the way you are motivated? What is it inside of you that produces the kinds of words that pour out of your mouth and the kinds of actions that your hands perform? It is the inner life, the heart, and that is what needs to be changed, says Jesus. This planning and motivational center of your being must be transformed so that you can begin to do things that please God and that benefit your neighbor. Until that takes place, you haven't begun to change at a level of depth.

And of course, nobody can learn to love God and learn to love his neighbor as he should until he has first come to know the love of Jesus Christ for him. It simply can't be done. "We love," says John in his first letter, "because *He first* loved us." And it is only when we come to a recognition of our sin and when we come to a relationship with Jesus Christ through faith in Him that transforms us and changes us to be different people *within,* that we can become different people *without.* This is the work of the Spirit of God. Look at Romans 5:5: "God's love has been poured into our hearts through the Holy Spirit Who was given to us." You can't love others, you can't love God until the Holy Spirit has been poured into - what? Your feelings? No. Until He is poured into your heart—i.e., your being—to change and transform and mold and remake the inner structure of your thought life. It was corrupted and twisted and warped through Adam's sin. So that's where you must begin. Without that kind of a viewpoint about counseling, you might as well not even start to think about changing people, because all you're going to do is to exchange one bad set of behavior patterns for another. You're not going to do anything at the level where it needs to be done - at the inner core of the human personality.

When the Spirit of God changes hearts, his inner alterations lead to a change of outward actions and life relationships. There isn't time to go into that in detail; I'm still in the introduction. But you can read about it in Romans 8: 10, 11; Romans 6:2, 19; Galatians 5—how the Spirit of God enables believers to transform the habit patterns of the "members" of the "body" by changing their hearts (for more on this, see *The Use of Scripture in Counseling*).

If you stress outward change, as so many people do, what happens? You will develop a legalistic liberalism: "Do this, don't do that." The notion will get abroad that you can change people by changing from the outside, their environment, or their behavior patterns. This legalistic liberal approach really says, "The cross is not necessary; all you have to do is obey the rules." We are not liberals; we believe the Bible and that the cross is the essential message that every Christian must proclaim. We are not legalistic; we believe that a man must operate out of love, not out of rules imposed upon him, that he is crammed into, and to which he has no commitment whatever. A person obeys His rules because he wants to please a God who had sent His Son to die for him. That makes all the difference in the world—and out of it!

On the other hand, if you stress the inner change alone and forget that the inner change leads to outward changes in behavior patterns as Romans 6, 7 and 8 tell us, then you get a cold orthodoxy that is great on doctrine, but doesn't do much to bring about changes in people's lives in any significant sense. They get all of this information tightly packed into their skulls, but it never gets into the fabric of everyday living. They do not walk in the truth, as the Scriptures beautifully put it, when with perfect balance they combine the inner/ outer sides of changed living. So it is absolutely essential to see that inner change is essential, but also that it leads to outer change. Those two sides are part and parcel of one another. If there is really no outer change—none whatsoever—there has been no inner change. If there are no works, there's no faith. But if there is minimal change (as there so often is), it may indicate that there hasn't been much good counseling; there has only been evangelism.

Now that's the first presupposition that I want to get across: counseling must be done on a level of depth, a level deep enough to transform the human heart. That fact makes a tremendous difference when you're counseling an unbeliever.

There are limits when counseling an unbeliever

The second fact grows out of the first: you must recognize the limitations that exist when counseling an unbeliever. First of all, unbelievers do not know Jesus Christ, and they do not care about knowing Jesus Christ in any significant way. So anything you say to them about obeying, loving, or serving Jesus Christ falls on deaf ears. The difference is explained in John 3:19-21:

> *And this is the judgment: . . . the Light has come into the world, but men loved darkness rather than the Light because their works were evil. Everyone who practices evil hates the Light and doesn't come to the Light so that his works won't be exposed. But whoever does the truth comes to the Light so that it may be clearly seen that his works have been carried out for God.*

In 1 Corinthians 12:3, Paul puts it this way:

> *I want you to understand that nobody who is speaking by God's Spirit ever says, 'Jesus be cursed.' And nobody can say 'Jesus is Lord,' except by the Holy Spirit.*

Now, Paul doesn't mean that a person can't utter the words with his lips hypocritically! Of course many thousands of people have done so, and there could be people right here who have fooled others around them because they have done just that. But they've repeated words that they don't really mean. They are not subject to Christ as Lord. Pushed on this question, Paul would say, "Nobody can say this *from his heart.*"

When the Bible speaks about believing something "with all your heart" or saying something "from the heart," what it means is that you're not just saying it with your lips. It is the *lips* and the heart that are contrasted in Scripture, not the *mind* and the heart. We talk about head-knowledge vs. heart-knowledge. That's not a biblical contrast. It's lips and heart that are contrasted; what we speak and what we believe (the contrast is between the inner and the outer man). To speak of doing something from the heart is to talk about sincerity, not about feelings over against intellectual thought. The contrast is between sincerity and hypocrisy. There may be someone here who has said, "Jesus is Lord" with his lips and never said it with his heart. The man who believes in his *heart* that God has raised Christ from the dead shall be saved. It must be genuine; it's got to come from the core of the being, from the inner person before God and before yourself. This says that no man can say "Jesus Christ is Lord" that way *until the Spirit of God has enabled him to do so.*

If that is true, how are we ever going to get people to change in counseling if they can't say, "Jesus is Lord"? If they can't say, "Jesus is Lord," they can't obey, they can't follow Him, they can't be His disciples.

You say, "What are you doing? It sounds as though you're proving that it's impossible to counsel unbelievers." Well, just hold on for a little bit. Please be patient.

Let me go one step further. Unbelievers can't understand the Scriptures either. Remember, we're trying to face the limitations honestly. In the second chapter of I Corinthians—among other startling things in that chapter—Paul says in the fourteenth and fifteenth verses:

> *But a natural person does not welcome the teachings of God's Spirit; they are foolishness to him and he is not able to know about them because they must be investigated spiritually. But the spiritual person is able to investigate everything while (on the other hand) no one has the ability to investigate him.*

What is a natural person? Just a plain old natural person, nothing has happened to him; he's just the way he was born by nature and that's it. He has never been transformed to any level of depth; he's just a natural person who has been born once with a sinful nature that can do only those things that displease God. A natural person is one who does not have the Spirit of love poured into his heart, so he cannot love God and his neighbor, and he does not welcome the teachings of God's Spirit.

Suppose you try to do biblical counseling with an unbeliever. You say, "There's a solution to your problem," and you turn to the Bible and tell him, "Here's what God says in His Word." What's his response? He says, "Huh!" He says (in effect), "So what?" And if he doesn't say "Huh!" out loud, he goes out and lives "Huh!" He doesn't *welcome* the teachings of God's Spirit. Why? The passage goes on to say, "They are foolishness to him and he is unable to know about them because they must be investigated spiritually." He does not have the ability to investigate the Bible on his own. He has only natural equipment with which to investigate it. He has his own nature, his own abilities, his own insights, and his own strength to do it. But this equipment won't do. To investigate Scripture properly takes something more, and he doesn't have what it takes to really understand that Book.

What is it that he needs? He can't investigate these things because they must be investigated spiritually. When the Spirit of God comes into a person's life through regeneration, he enables that person to read the Bible with new eyes and to understand it with a new mind. He transforms the person so that he comes to the Book with a new heart, and he begins to see things that he never saw there before. Have you ever talked to an unbeliever who says, "Aw, the Bible -that's a dead book"? I've heard that dozens of times from unbelievers. And I say to them, "No, you're a dead person, the Book is alive." You get the same effect, whether the book is dead or the person is dead. Because he doesn't have spiritual life, the life that the Spirit of God gives to enable one to understand this book, it is dead to him.

Think of a corpse lying up here in a casket. We could gather to eat the most delicious meal you have ever tasted—mountains of potatoes, lakes of gravy, fields of green peas, and forests of roast beef reaching towards the sky. The aroma could fill this whole huge auditorium. And then we could bring a dessert that looks like Niagaras of whipped cream cascading over cliffs of apricots. And we bring this huge, magnificent meal to the corpse, and say, "Here it is! Look at it! Ah, doesn't it get to you? Not a shiver. Not even a sniff. Why? Because that body is dead. It is insensitive to the aromas, the beauty, the magnificence, the taste, and everything else. Here, in this Book, is a far more wonderful meal. God said that we can't live by bread alone, so He gave us His Word. But everywhere there are spiritual corpses walking around who don't know Jesus Christ, who have no spiritual life, and who can't appreciate it. And are you, as a counselor, going to change them by using the Word of God? Are you going to tell them what they should do to get their three squares for that day so that they can live by God's Word? No! They won't have any part of it; that is what it says here. They don't welcome it; they aren't able to know about it, because they can't investigate the Bible spiritually. The Spirit of God must first come into a person's life and enable him to get excited about this book for it to come alive to him.

Now I Corinthians 2 goes on to say, "The spiritual person," that is, the person who has the Spirit of God in his life, "is able to investigate everything while (on the other hand) no one has the ability to investigate him." The unbeliever can't understand the believer. He sees him as a strange character. He looks at him and says, "I don't understand him." He talks about varieties of religious experience, the psychology of conversion and all these things, but it's all off base. When you read such things, you laugh and cry, because you know that they come nowhere near the truth. Unbelievers can't understand why you do what you do, why you don't do what you don't do, why you take an interest in a prayer meeting and sing in a choir. They don't understand any of these things. They can't. It takes the Spirit of God living in a man to enable him to understand. So the unbeliever isn't going to understand and appreciate the Christian counselor either.

Right here in this room tonight are all kinds of things that you don't see or hear, but they are here. There are all sorts of pictures—beer advertisements, commercials, etc., and all kinds of music—rock and roll, popular, classical—right here, right now. You didn't know that, did you?

"Right here in the First Baptist Church in Atlanta?" Yes, they are here. I could bring in a television set and turn it on and let you see and hear it all. It would all take place right here because those sounds and those pictures are all around us in this room. We don't hear them. Why? Because we don't have a receiving set, and we're probably just as well off that we don't! But that's the way the unbeliever is when it comes to the Word of God and the things of God. Listen to what Paul says, in verse 9, "What *eye* hasn't seen and *ear* hasn't heard"—that's just like the absence of that television set; without it, you can't see and can't hear. Let's go on "... and hasn't been conceived by the human heart, is what God has prepared for those who love Him. And to us God has revealed it by His Spirit." That's what we must realize: that poor, unsaved fellow who sits in front of you in the counselee's seat seeking help can't see or hear.

How are you going to help him? If you (as a good biblical counselor) turn to the Scriptures and advise him, he can't even get it. Your words and the Bible's words are sounds coming through the air, but he doesn't have the receiving equipment to pick them up. That's what it is like when you use the Word of God to counsel an unbeliever. You have to get that clear. There are serious limitations in counseling an unbeliever. It is essential to recognize that.

"Well," you say, "Things are going from bad to worse. It looks as though it is utterly hopeless to try to counsel an unbeliever. Would you please get to what I *can* do? I thought you were going to talk about how to counsel." Now, please be patient. I have just a bit more to say first.

Now we have seen that unbelievers don't have the power to understand the Scriptures, but that isn't all—there is still another limitation. Even if they *were* able to understand the Scriptures, even if they wanted to obey the Scriptures and obey Christ, they couldn't because *they don't have the power of the Holy Spirit* to enable them to obey. I don't have time to get into it, but look at the third chapter of Paul's letter to the Galatians, where he reminds them that you must begin the Christian life by grace through faith, by God's doing everything for you in Christ - you cannot save yourself. Then Paul asks them, "What is wrong with you; beginning by grace, do you think you now are going to grow by your own strength?" The implied response is "absolutely not." The only way a

Christian can grow is if the Spirit of God continues to change him and make him different in the days to come. So, what are we going to do for unbelieving counselees?

There is no holiness apart from the power of the Spirit, giving us strength to obey God's Word. Now, there is a very important point to get clear about this. People today are teaching false doctrine that sounds good. I am saying just as clearly as I know how that we cannot depend on our own strength to make changes that please God. That's what I've been saying all along. The Spirit of God must enable us to understand the Word, must give us the power to obey the Word, and must give us the ability to declare Jesus Christ as our Lord and to really live as His servants.

So, since this is true some say, "That means that I must do nothing, absolutely nothing. All I do is give up. All I do is recede into the background, and the less there is of me and the less there is even of my obedience or efforts or anything else, the more there will be of the Holy Spirit." And that sounds good, doesn't it? And it is, if you interpret that rightly, but it isn't, if you interpret that wrongly. And they are interpreting it wrongly; they are interpreting it as passivity.

A Christian must obey God. A Christian must believe that the Holy Spirit does not do the believing for us, and the Holy Spirit does not do the obeying for us. We are responsible beings who are going to be held responsible for believing and doing what God says, but we dare not do the obeying or believing *in our own strength*. We must rely upon the strength of the Holy Spirit. That's the point. It is the Spirit who enables us to believe, and it is the Spirit who enables us to obey. We must not try to do these things in our own strength, or we shall do them wrongly. But this is crucial—we must do them. He doesn't do them for us, as some are teaching. So, then, you've got to recognize these limitations when trying to help an unbeliever.

Never Settle for Anything Less than Real Change

"Well then, if we can't counsel him at a level of depth and make those kinds of changes, what can we do for him? I guess we'll have to settle for something less." *No! Never!* No, you can settle for nothing less than changing him at a level of depth. "But we can't change him at a level of depth. You yourself said so. He won't listen to us; he won't listen to the Word; he has no power; he does not have the Spirit; he's a natural man; he does not have the receiving set; all of these things are impossible! How are we going to do what we can't do?" That's the dilemma.

But before we try to solve that dilemma, let me make it very clear that you may not settle for something less. You *must* not settle for something less. You cannot do band-aid work when your counselee needs radical surgery. You dare not. That's the most cruel and heartless thing a person could possibly do. When someone goes to a surgeon and says, "I think I have cancer," the surgeon puts him through all the tests. If the surgeon knows in his heart that this man has cancer, and that unless he operates on him, the man is going to die within a year, what does he do, settle for something less? Does that surgeon say, "I just can't bring myself to tell this man this terrible news. I want to make him happy, and I don't want to be unhappy myself. I don't want him to be upset with me. I don't want to see him cry; I don't want his wife to cry, I want him to leave here happy. 'Here, sir, is a salve that you can put on that sore.'" If he says that, the surgeon makes the man happy, and the surgeon feels better too, because he didn't have to go through the cancer scene. But when the man realizes six months later that there is no hope because the surgeon didn't do the hard thing that he should have done, then that man hates the surgeon, and the surgeon feels worse. The man may even sue the surgeon for incompetence. The same is true for you—you must not give Band-Aids to people with cancer. You must not say to an unbeliever, "Look, let's change a few superficial things and settle for that." God hasn't called us to reform people. That's always the beginning of liberalism—when people settle for something less than a change at a level of depth, a change in the heart of a man.

And if we did settle for something less, if we did settle for changing a few outward things, shifting certain patterns of life here and substituting patterns of life there; if we did settle for something on that level, what would we settle for? We would settle for misrepresenting God's whole message and mission in sending Christ. We would say (in effect) that the cross is a cruel mockery; a farce, a ridiculous waste.

And we would say to people by that, "God has a way to change your life without Christ. You don't need to trust Him as Savior." And that would misrepresent God.

Moreover, we would foster thereby a false assurance in unbelievers. We would lead them to think that they were all right with God when they were not. Pretty soon they would be let down hard when the new patterns turned out to be no better than the former. Then they would think that God let them down. No, we dare not settle for something less.

"What then can you do for an unbeliever? It looks as though you can't counsel him." You're right. That's what I've been telling you. You can't counsel an unbeliever; no, you can't. You've been concluding that all along, and I agree with you; you can't counsel an unbeliever. There's no way to counsel an unbeliever. Now I'm not going to walk off the platform at that point and leave you there. You can't counsel an unbeliever if you mean by counseling what the Bible means by counseling—changing him at a level of depth. The man won't listen because his heart is not oriented toward the Book, so he can't hear what it has to say, and he doesn't have the power to obey the Book, even if he wanted to. You can't counsel an unbeliever in the full biblical sense of that word "counsel." What then can you do for an unbeliever?

Well, there are some things that you can do for an unbeliever, so long as you make it clear all along that you haven't started counseling yet. Continually, as you work with an unbeliever, you've got to make it evident to him that anything and everything that you're doing before he comes to know Jesus Christ as his Savior is not counseling; it's not what God is offering to people as the remedy for their problems. It is something introductory to what will bring about this greater thing (if indeed he comes to know Christ).

What you do then is preliminary; it is pre-counseling. And that is all that you can do for an unbeliever; you pre-counsel him, but you can't really counsel him. And all that pre-counseling means is that you are going to do some problem-oriented evangelism. That's what pre-counseling is—*problem-oriented evangelism*. That's what you can do for an unbeliever. Now, how do you do problem-oriented evangelism?

Problem-Oriented Evangelism

There are many things I could say about that, but I shall mention only a few. Jesus helped many people, sometimes with superficial problems on a superficial basis first, but always in connection with evangelism. When healing bodies, for example, He always connected the greater healing of the eyes of the heart, or the paralysis of the heart, or the leprosy of the heart with the physical healing. That's just what you must do in counseling. You must approach unbelievers with both hands. You have something in both hands to offer: on one hand, something very minimal, and on the other, the entrance into real counseling, which changes at a level of depth that begins with the gospel of the Lord Jesus Christ.

This involves three things that I will quickly mention. **First**, it means removing obstacles to a presentation of the gospel. The phone rings. The pastor picks it up. What does he hear at the other end? *"All right pastor, this fine Christian wife of mine has her bags packed. What are you going to do about it?"* Is that the time to evangelize Joe? Hardly. What you say is, "Joe, put Mary on the phone." He gets Mary to the phone and you say, "Mary, we've talked about I Corinthians 7 many times before. It says that if your husband wants to stay with you, even if he is an unbeliever, you are to make as good a marriage out of that marriage as you possibly can. You are to do everything you can do as a believer. You are to really hang in there, you're to try to win him and your children to the Lord Jesus Christ. Now, packing your bags and threatening to leave him is sin. This is wrong, and you *know* it's wrong. So get those bags unpacked, and you and Joe get over here as fast as you can. I'm going to a funeral in twenty minutes." (You know, a funeral comes before anything else.) So, Mary grudgingly says, "All right."

Ten minutes later she gets there with Joe. You have ten minutes left. Joe comes in feeling a little better, but he is still upset. He doesn't know what is going to happen. And you get him in there. Is that the time to evangelize?

Absolutely not. You have ten minutes. You're under pressure to go to a funeral. What do you do? You say, "Look, Joe, Mary, I just want two fur-lined, ironclad promises out of you. First of all Mary, I want you to promise that you won't threaten Joe with this sin again. We've got to get this out of the picture. And secondly, I want a promise from both of you that you'll be here at 7:00 tonight. We're going to start counseling to find out what is going wrong in this marriage and what God says can be done about it."

If the pastor can get them to make those commitments, he's done some pretty good pre-counseling. He's done a few things minimally to help them, but he hasn't really done any counseling yet (except possibly with Mary). When Joe and Mary come back at 7:00 and he begins to talk to them, it is possible that he can begin to evangelize Joe. So you see, sometimes there are obstacles to the presentation of the gospel. When a man is all upset about his wife with her bags packed, and she's heading for the airport, that's no time to talk to him about the Lord. You had better stop her first; then he might listen. Often, you have to do pre-counseling of that sort.

Secondly, sometimes you have to give pre-counseling hope to those who have lost it, by making certain minimal efforts. In the case of the man born blind recorded in John 9, Jesus put clay on his eyes. It wasn't Jesus' saliva that healed him; there was nothing mystical or medicinal about it. It wasn't the clay on his eyes that healed him either; neither of those things had anything to do with the healing. Christ's action was designed to give him hope. Here was a man who was born blind; he had no hope of ever seeing. Nobody ever heard of a blind man seeing. But when Jesus put the clay on his eyes, He gave him hope. The man began to think: "If only I could wash my blindness away as I can wash off that clay, I could see." Hope began to well up within him, for the first time, perhaps, since he long ago laid aside any hope of such a miracle taking place. And Jesus at that moment said, "Go wash in the pool of Siloam," and the man went and washed, and came back seeing. He wouldn't have gone if Jesus hadn't given him hope. He would have said, "This is foolishness." Sometimes you have to give hope by doing something for somebody first.

Thirdly, you have to approach each person differently. Jesus approached Nicodemus quite differently from the way he approached the woman at the well. Nicodemus comes and says, "We know that you are a teacher come from God because no man is able to do these miracles unless God is with him." And Jesus said, picking up on his very phrase, "No man *is able* to enter the kingdom of God unless he is born again." Nicodemus comes and says, "I want to talk about theology." Jesus says, "I want to talk about your life." *Pow!* Right smack in the teeth. That was a "Brother, are you saved?" evangelism approach (without the "brother") if there ever was one. There were teeth lying all around the room when He was done with Nicodemus.

But look at the woman at the well. It was supremely gradual; He led her through buckets, ropes, husbands, and hills. She says, "Oh, you're a teacher," then she says, "You're a prophet," and at last, "You're the Messiah!" He leads her there very gradually. With the blind man, He didn't even talk to him about salvation at first; He just healed him and disappeared. People came to him and said, "You're in cahoots with that man Jesus." But he answered, "This one thing I know. A man named Jesus made clay, put it on my eyes, sent me to the pool, and I came back seeing." His parents came to him and he told them, "This one thing I know … "The Pharisees came to him and he said, "This one thing I know …" and he told them the same story all over again. They threw him out of the synagogue, but he still protested all the way to the doorstep, "This one thing I know… "Why? Because that's all he knew. That's all he knew. Jesus hadn't told him another thing. It was only on the next encounter that Jesus talked to him about the blindness of the heart, the inner life.

All three situations differed, but there is one thing that is true of every one of them—the same message of Jesus Christ's death on that cross in the place of guilty sinners, and His bodily resurrection from the dead. That's the good news. Paul puts it very plainly in 1 Corinthians 15: "This is the good news that I preached to you, by which you are saved." There is only one good news, one message: Christ died for our sins according to the Scriptures; He was buried and He rose the third day according to the Scriptures. These two facts were predicted in the Old Testament Scriptures: the death of Christ for sinners and His bodily resurrection from the dead. Go through the whole book of Acts and look up every time somebody in the book of Acts preached the gospel or talked to somebody about the Lord, and always the death and resurrection will appear. The death and resurrection, the penal, substitutionary death and bodily resurrection of Christ—that's the good news. That's what Jesus, all the Apostles, and everybody else proclaimed. In evangelism, that is what you must call all men to believe.

In closing, let me suggest three approaches that you might use in dealing with people who need pre-counseling. When you have given certain pre-counseling help, you might point out where the pre-counseling came from and why you were motivated to help Joe get his wife back from the airport. And you can stress what it was that motivated her to come back. This woman agreed to stay home and unpack her bags only because there was an authority over her life, an authority that brought order and change into her life, even at that point.

I had a couple in counseling one time where the wife sat down, and the husband wouldn't. He was storming all over the place and stomping around. Between his expletives, I patched this story together. He said, "My wife is a Christian and I'm not, and she knew I didn't want to come to a Christian counselor. She deceived me. She said, 'We're going for counseling,' but she didn't tell me it was *Christian* counseling, and I'm mad." (He didn't have to mention the last fact.)

When I heard his story, I began to talk to her, but I just let him go stomping around. I turned to her and said, "Is this true? Are you really a Christian?" She gave some evidence of really believing. Then I said, "Now what he says about you, is this true—that you deceived him and so on?" She said, "Yeah, he wouldn't have come any other way." So I ignored him and began to give her a little mini-sermon, to show her from the Scriptures that this was sin. I began to show her from I Peter 3 that she had dishonored God, she had lied to her husband, she had not been submissive to him, etc. About halfway through that mini-sermon he began to calm down and listen, looking at her and looking at me. Next thing you know, he was standing still and edging over, listening. Then, he sat down on the chair and put his elbow down on the desk, listening. Before long he said, "Give it to her." Now there was a fellow who was getting hope. You must understand that he had a long way to go; this was still pre-counseling. But he got enough hope from it to stay throughout all the counseling sessions to come. Why? Because, as he said, for the first time, somebody somewhere could control his wife! And I made it clear to him that it was the Holy Spirit who controlled her through this Book. It wasn't I. She wasn't listening to me. She wouldn't have cared any more for what I said than she did for what he said. But she had a basic commitment to Jesus Christ, and He was controlling her life, in spite of her feelings. Her husband didn't come to know Christ in these sessions as I counseled his wife, but that woman, since then, has really become what she ought to be, and I believe that if she continues to live this way, she herself may lead him to Christ.

So, one thing to point out is where the pre-counseling help comes from. Secondly, there is a point at which you have to say in pre-counseling, "Whoa!" (One of the greatest words in counseling is "Whoa!" When I was in Germany recently I even got the Germans saying "Whoa!" in counseling.) Use your own words, I don't care what they are, but there is a place where you have to bring pre-counseling to a screeching halt and say, "This is as far as it can go." There comes a time when you've done all the pre-counseling, you've given all the help you can give, and then you have to say to the unbeliever that if he doesn't trust Christ, after you've been talking to him about the gospel, "We're up against a brick wall. I want to give you real counseling. I want you to experience all the changes that the Holy Spirit can make in a person's life." And you can even describe them. Then you can say, "I'd like to do all these things for you, but we're up against a brick wall because all those things are on the other side of the wall and you're on this side. There is only one way to get through it—through the Door, through the One who said, 'I am the Door.'" You can describe what you'd really like to see happen, and how you would like to counsel at a level of depth, but you can take him only to that point in pre-counseling. Then you tell him, "I can do no more for you until you go through that Door."

I've often said to people at that point, "Look, if you came to my house and you didn't bother to ring the doorbell or knock on the door or anything, but you just opened the door and walked in, and then you walked into my kitchen and opened my refrigerator door, and you made yourself whatever you liked (a big ham sandwich or whatever) and you munched away at that and drank a nice big glass of Coke or Pepsi and then you said, 'Well, I'm feeling better, but I'm a bit sleepy,' so you marched upstairs and slept in my bed, like the Three Bears story, would you expect me to protest, or do you think I'd be happy to let this go on?"

"Why not? Because you're not a member of the family. If my children walk through the door without knocking, they have a perfect right to, I don't expect them to knock every time they come to my front door. I even give them keys.

My wife can come in too; I never expect her to knock on the door. She can sleep in my bed, etc. (Now I do draw the line at my toothbrush.) Why can they do all these things and you can't? Because they are part of the family. God has provided biblical counseling for His children, which is at a level of depth. But not for others. You can have all the wonderful promises of the Scriptures if you become a member of the family, but now you're not a member of the family." I turn to John 1:12 and read," 'As many as received Him, to *them* gave He the right to become children of God.' You must receive Him first by faith. That comes first. All of this is on the other side of the brick wall, and Christ is the Door."

Now, let me say one more thing in closing about what to do if he doesn't believe, if he won't pay attention to your pre-counseling. You can do a lot of things, of course, but there is one thing I've done that God has blessed in a number of situations, although not uniformly. Not everybody believed when Jesus Christ spoke to them, and it's not always your fault if people will not believe you when you talk to them. It may be your fault, of course; it was never Christ's fault. You have only two problems, and I have two problems; He had only one: people, not Himself. Our problem is that we have to check out whether we did the right thing, as well as whether or not the person did the right thing. With Christ, the play was a success, but the audience was a failure. So, you have to keep that in mind too.

But what if a person won't believe? What if you've checked yourself and you believe under God that you've done the best you can, and it really is his rebellious attitude toward the gospel? Well, you conclude that you can lead a horse to water, but you can't make him drink. And you repeat all through that last session (as it becomes apparent that this will be the last)—I try to weave it in twenty times and even write it down on a piece of paper, if possible—a verse that he can carry with him. I try to indelibly impress it upon him so that he'll never forget it. All through that last session I quote Proverbs 13:15. It's short, it's to the point, and it's memorable. I say, "Well, if you're not going to believe this message, I want you to remember that God says, 'the way of the transgressor is hard.' And when you get out there and start facing this problem or that and such and such a thing happens, you're going to find out that 'the way of the transgressor is hard.' Remember that if such and such a thing happens, that's when I'd like you to think about the fact that 'the way of the transgressor is hard.'" I keep saying it and saying it, and saying it. And I've had people come back in six months and I've asked them, "What has brought you back here?" "I've found out that the way of the transgressor is hard." I think you have to put a burr under his saddle. The best burr I know is the Scriptures.

Let me say it once more: you can't counsel unbelievers in the biblical sense of the word (changing them, sanctifying them through the work of the Holy Spirit, as His Word is ministered to their hearts) so long as they remain unbelievers. The change they need is the regenerating work of the Holy Spirit. So do pre-counseling: present the gospel, and pray that the Holy Spirit will open their hearts to receive it in faith. Evangelism is essential. That must come first.

The Influence of Westminster[1]

As solid evidence as anyone could wish for the significant influence of the Westminster Standards is the presence of the many delegates meeting here after 350 years. You, yourselves, gathered in this place to commemorate the writing of these memorable documents, are living proof of their lasting influence. Indeed, there is almost nothing more left to be said that you have not already affirmed by your happy attendance at these meetings. My purpose, then, is to help record the remarkable fact that we meet at this time to bear witness to the fact that the faith of Westminster is still alive and well in our day.

Over the intervening years, between the writing of the Westminster documents and the present time, they have received innumerable accolades from friend and foe alike. Philip Schaff called Westminster the "first among Protestant councils," and declared that the Westminster Confession is the "fullest and ripest symbolic statement of the Calvinistic system of doctrine." He went on to say that it had "as much vitality as any of the Protestant symbols and more vitality than most of them." In discussing their form, he wrote, "The style of the Confession and Catechisms is clear, strong, dignified, and well adapted to the grave subject."

More recently, Loraine Boettner wrote, "Calvinism finds its most perfect expression in the Westminster Confession." Concerning the Assembly that produced it, he declared, "whether judged by the extent and ability of its labors, or by its influence upon later generations, it stands first among Protestant councils." As "the creed of the church," he

---

[1] This was the closing address delivered to the Assembly of the North American Presbyterian and Reformed Counsel (NAPARC) meeting on the occasion of the 350th anniversary of the Westminster Assembly.

claims, "every line sustains a courageous stand" for truth. He also noted, "In these standards we have the grandest conception of theological truth that has ever entered the mind of man. As a system it exhibits far more depth of theological insight than does any other, and it is worthy of the admiration of the ages." B. B. Warfield's assessment was that it is "the most complete, the most fully elaborated and carefully guarded, the most perfect, and the most vital expression that has ever been framed by the hand of man, of all that enters into what we call evangelical religion, and of all that must be safeguarded if evangelical religion is to persist in the world." Alexander Cheyne speaks of its "long career of a shaping influence in the life of both the church and the [Scottish] nation," while John Leith notes that the "influence of the Westminster Confession and Catechisms in the shaping of American life has been very great." Sydney Ahlstrom has estimated that "three-fourths of the American people in 1776 had been significantly influenced by the Puritan and Reformed type of Protestantism" saying, "the influence of the Westminster Assembly on the creative religious movements of the frontier defies calculation." A. C. Heron's studied conclusion is that "it has been unusually widely influential .. . through the last three and one half centuries."

Even its foes have had to recognize the significance of the Westminster Standards. Robert Baillie wrote in 1647, "The Confession is much cried up by all, even many of our greatest opposites, as the best confession yet extant." Milton, a bitter foe of historic Christianity, while criticizing the Assembly, had to admit that it was a "learned and memorable synod" in which "piety, learning, and prudence were housed." Dr. Curry, former editor of the Methodist Advocate, in an editorial on creeds, called the Westminster Confession "the ablest, clearest, and most comprehensive system of Christian doctrine ever framed-a wonderful monument to the intellectual greatness of its framers." Dean Stanley, no advocate of its teachings, said, "it far more nearly approaches the full proportions of a theological treatise, and exhibits far more depth of theological insight, than any other" (emphasis added).

Yet while receiving such fulsome praise, when judged by the purpose for which it was convened, the Westminster Assembly was a failure. This Assembly, called together by Parliament to standardize the doctrine, worship, and discipline of three kingdoms, did not realize that end. Some of those who labored until 1648, five-and-one-half years after the Assembly was convened, must have been greatly disappointed that in the succeeding years this purpose was not achieved. It must have seemed that their labor was largely in vain—that the project failed to attain its major goals. However, in his wise providence, God had other purposes in mind. Judged by his providential purposes, as they have worked out throughout the years, it is evident that our great God planned to achieve far more, on a wider scale than its framers imagined.

The Westminster Assembly was unique. Never before or since have so many devoted, competent Christian scholars gathered together for so long a period of time to define so many crucial teachings of the faith so well. The work of such a gathering, one would suppose, could not be without great influence. And indeed, for 350 years, the impact of what was done here has been felt not only in England, Scotland, and Ireland, but also in the United States, Canada, Australia, South Africa, and wherever else English-speaking peoples live.

In God's providence, it is significant that the Westminster Standards were composed in English—a language that subsequently has become the language of the world, the new *koine*, the *lingua franca* of our time. Consequently, wherever English is spoken, these standards are immediately accessible in their original form.

The influence of portions of these Standards, particularly portions of the Shorter Catechism, extends far beyond Presbyterians to churches whose doctrinal positions are in many ways incompatible with the Reformed faith. In fact, not only doctrinal friends, but others, quote sections as if they were part of their own confessions. How is that? For one thing, in many places, the wording of some catechetical answers has become the classic statement of that truth for all Christians. Take, for example, Question Fourteen: "What is Sin?" The answer to which is, "Sin is any want of conformity unto, or transgression of, the law of God." Than that succinct, but comprehensive statement, it would be difficult to imagine finer wording. Consider, too, the great and perhaps even better-known response to Question One, "What is the chief end of man? Man's chief end is to glorify God and to enjoy him forever."

I have asked diverse groups of pastors—from a large variety of backgrounds—"What is the chief end of man?" Without hesitation, the answer is "to glorify God, and to enjoy him forever." There is something significant about that. People with Calvinistic, Arminian, as well as nondescript theologies, unite in that great affirmation in the words of the Westminster Shorter Catechism. That fact says something about its powerful influence upon the Church of Jesus Christ.

Today, in many ways, while affirming the truth taught in the Catechism, the church is departing from it in practice. Christians—perhaps more than ever before—need to understand what those words mean in everyday actions. Listen to any discussion about the problems of believers, or read the average book from the shelf of a Christian bookstore and you will discover that—far from glorifying God—advice is given about the chief end of man that flatly contradicts the Catechism. While writers usually do not begin with the statement, "Man's chief end is ..." nevertheless, their statements assert that man's purpose in life is "to find happiness," or "to feel good about himself," or "to obtain security and significance." Clearly, there is something quite different about the orientation of those answers. Nowhere does the Bible or the Westminster Standards teach any such thing.

What is the problem? You can see what has gone wrong by comparing the Catechism's response with the answers listed above. In one case, the response is God-directed; in the other, it is man-directed. In the one case, God is the object of life; in the other, man.

Today is a time of unparalleled self-centeredness. Humanistic philosophy has permeated the church, so that the dominant concern is no longer to glorify God but to become self-actualized. It is therefore time to re-emphasize the truth taught in Question One: Man's chief end, not his only end, but his chief end, is to glorify God and enjoy him forever.

Note well that the Catechism answer does not say "Glorify God, and enjoy the world—or yourself—forever." It does not say that man's purpose is enjoyment. What it says is that man should enjoy GOD. We are to have an enjoyment of his being, his works, his word—the kind of enjoyment found in the hymns of the psalmists. Man is not capable of finding true, lasting joy in perishable things or in associations with other sinful creatures. It is only in fellowship with God, who made us, that we experience such joy. Even that, as the Catechism seems to say, is derivative—a by-product—of glorifying God.

What does it mean to glorify God? The Old Testament Hebrew word for glory is "weight, heaviness." The New Testament term is "fame." Paul, in II Corinthians 4:17, brings them both together when he speaks of the heavenly "weight of glory" that awaits those who, like him, glorify God. When the Old Testament idea of glory-as-weight is examined, the idea of giving God his proper weight in all things is uppermost. God is to be honored for all his works and for all he is. He is to be acknowledged as the one who sustains the world and all that is in it. That note is missing in today's society, a society in which people are caught up in themselves. It is a rare thing for anyone on television, in a newspaper account, or anywhere else, to give God the glory for his accomplishments. Today, man is willing to take the credit for everything. God, if considered at all, is considered a light-weight. He has all but been driven from public life. Even privately, the average person lives his life from year to year without ever thinking of God. God has become irrelevant.

The New Testament concept of glory-as-fame accords with the idea of glory-as-weight. When God is given his rightful place (weight), his fame is spread abroad among men. It is this emphasis, so strongly taught in years past when children were reared on the Shorter Catechism, that is so greatly needed. Many problems now prevalent in the church would evaporate if believers would once more take this matter to heart. As Presbyterians who love our Standards, let us heed the answer to the first question of the Catechism, and learn afresh to enjoy God as we glorify him in all that we do! Perhaps, then, not only the works but also the joyful Christian life implied in the answer will begin to spread to people of all theological persuasions.

While the Westminster Standards have had a universal impact upon all forms of English-speaking Christianity, arguably, the greatest influence they have exerted is upon churches that have espoused them as their secondary standards. Not only have they provided identity and stability as a means of maintaining the faith once delivered to the saints, enabling them to hold fast to the "form of doctrine" they have received, but these documents also have been a filtering factor, straining out heresy and unbelief. It is upon these two influences—unity and discrimination—that we shall now focus in conclusion.

First, consider the unifying influence of the Westminster Standards. The idea of drawing up a Confession, complete with catechisms, that would unify was part of the original intention in calling the Assembly. The commissioners knew this from the beginning and attempted to produce documents that would achieve this end, spending long, arduous hours at the task. To a great extent, their thorough efforts were rewarded.

Today, Presbyterian and Reformed denominations that comprise the North American Presbyterian and Reformed Council (NAPARC) have gathered to commemorate the 350th anniversary of the convening of the Westminster Assembly. Such a convention as this could take place only because of the mutual acceptance of, and adherence to, the Westminster documents. The meetings we have been holding here rightly attest to the unifying power of the Westminster Standards. By accepting these documents as their common confession, these churches have been able to maintain a basic unity of faith among themselves and among their individual congregations as well. Had there been no Standards, there would be no NAPARC; there would be no basis for unity. One can picture, instead, each denomination—indeed, each individual congregation—wandering off in a different direction.

As important as the unity of the faith may be, however, it is of equal importance to recognize the sifting, discriminating, and separating power that these documents possess. After all, as many have discovered to their peril, there can be no true unity where there is no unanimity of belief.

Discrimination, the ability to distinguish between things that differ, is the flip side of the unity coin. The same door that opens to invite some ministers and elders to enter shuts others out. The Westminster Standards do an admirable job of both. Arminian and Dispensationalist beliefs, as well as Arian and Unitarian, are excluded. Westminster's precise, in-depth statements of various biblical doctrines—often defined in minute detail—serve to separate those beliefs which are truly reformed from others.

Please note that this negative side has a positive effect. Standards that exclude eliminate those who would cause dissension and disunity. Yet Westminster maintains a proper and biblical catholicity that has always discouraged reformed churches from becoming isolated from other believers, or narrow in outlook. Reformed churches, adhering to the Standards, have always been at the forefront of unity and true, scriptural ecumenicity. Moreover, Presbyterians, who have continued to adhere to the Westminster teachings have been able to maintain a consistency of belief all over the world for 350 years.

Our Confession of Faith plainly recognizes all other evangelical denominations as part of the true Church, but most clearly declares our distinctive beliefs with a greater degree of biblical understanding than some confessions. This Confession is what a confession ought to be. A confession is, literally, a "saying together." Yes! It is a "saying together," in which we most joyfully join. Here—in this commemorative gathering that now draws to an end—how gladly we, in our generation, 350 years later, together with our godly forefathers, "say together," in one great affirmation, that we, too, adhere to the faith confessed therein.

The Biblical Perspectives on the Mind/Body Problem[1] Part One

The old ditty has it: "What is mind? No matter. Well, then, what is matter? Never mind." That's not very funny, but it's quite descriptive of our knowledge. That's about all that many Christians can say about the mind-body question: "Well, mind isn't body and body isn't mind." And yet, there is much more we need to say and many things we need to think about very seriously.

My intention is to move us a bit farther along the road to understanding in this area - not to complete the job but to move us somewhere beyond total ignorance. The title contains five important items. The **first** is *biblical*, *biblical* perspectives. That means that we're going to base our approach on Scripture. The Scriptures are the basis and ultimate authority for our conclusions. I shall presuppose the Scriptures as the inerrant Word of God, given as the infallible rule of faith and practice concerning everything of which the Scriptures wish to speak, not concerning everything, but everything that the Scriptures intend to teach. The Bible doesn't authoritatively tell us whether we ought to buy an American or Japanese car, for example.

The **second** word is *Perspectives*. The plural assumes that there is more than one, and I take this to mean ways in which the Bible looks at the question.

The **third** word is tough—*mind*. It is a word needing a Biblical definition because there are so many views that people hold that compete with

---

[1] Adapted from a presentation to the Winter Institute on Counseling in Medicine given in San Diego, February, 1992.

biblical concepts. For instance, Thomas Huxley once wrote, "Thought is as much a function of matter as motion is." Moreover, the vague notions that most Christians have when they use the word "mind" should be sharpened. The present view prevalent in our country today, and perhaps around the Western world at least, is very close to a complete somatizing of man—making him all body. Respac, for example, puts it this way:

> "Mind is nothing more than a term we employ to describe some of the functions of the brain."

We'll have to examine that idea in some detail as we go along. The **fourth** important word is *body*. We have to talk about the body because, significantly, the Bible does not distinguish the brain from the body. We must, therefore, understand as "body" everything that goes into the ground and rots, including the brain (Some brains, perhaps, rot before they go into the ground). With physicians, the definition might need to be altered to state that everything that goes into a jar of formalin is body.

Finally, there is the word *problem*. The problem to be addressed is the relationship of mind to body. What is this relationship, the nature of it, and what are the implications of that?

Body

The first point to discuss is how the Bible deals with the body. There are two principal terms for "body" in the Bible. One of these is soma. In the term "psychosomatics," the word psycho means "soul," and somatics means "body." In the Old Testament, the Hebrew word is *basar* ("flesh"), and its equivalent in the New Testament is *sarx*. *Sarcophagus*, for example, means a "flesh-eater". It is important to understand something of the use of these Scriptural words and something of the distinctions between them. "Body" speaks of this form that we know, that we see, that we touch, that we can feel. It often speaks of the form as a person. But, "flesh" means the living material of the body—the living material of this form and refers more to the composition of the body. "Flesh" also has the concept of weakness attached to it, which goes along with the concept of sin affecting and weakening our bodies. Sin makes our bodies incapable of completely doing what they were originally designed to do.

The body is respected in the Scriptures. Scripture repudiates the Gnostic idea that matter is evil. Gnosticism taught that spirit is good and matter is evil. Many harmful ideas came from this basic Gnostic teaching which early got a grip upon non-biblical thinkers. Gnosticism was already a problem in New Testament times. Two whole books were written just to refute Gnosticism—the book of Colossians and the book of First John. Remember the passage in First John that says Jesus came not only "by water" but also "by blood." The Gnostics taught that Christ was not really the one who died on that cross—that some phantom or someone resembling Christ (there were various views of how it happened) died on the cross, but that the Christ who came upon the man Jesus was separable from Him and that this Christ left Him before the cross. It came upon Him at the baptism (the "water") and left before the cross (the "blood"). But John says, "No, He's the one who came not only by water but also by blood." He was arguing that Jesus Christ was a real man with a real body and that it was that body that died.

We see, therefore, that this problem already began in New Testament times, and that New Testament writers fought gnosticism even in its early stages. As it grew much larger, many problems occurred in the Church. The Bible knows nothing of the body being evil. Matter was created by God and it was created good. When God finished creating matter, He looked upon creation and He said, "It's good. It's all very good."

The idea that the body is evil, therefore, is not Christian. It is not a Biblical, concept. The body, however, becomes a problem, as we'll see later on, because of the way the soul programs it. Also, the body is affected by the results of sin, including God's curse upon this world, so that the body does not function as it ought. While it is not evil itself, the effects of evil are clearly seen in the body. In fact, the body is looked upon so reverently in the Bible that it has to be buried. Not to be buried is considered a great insult. In Scripture, a dog eating an unburied body is the epitome of temporal judgment. The dogs in the city were the city street cleaners. When a body was just cast aside and not buried, and was eaten by dogs, that was a great disgrace. The ultimate insult to a living person was to call him a dog, because a dog was a scavenger.

The redeemed body is called the "temple of the Holy Spirit." I Corinthians 6:19, for example, contains a clear statement on that point. There God tells us how He looks upon the body of a redeemed saint. He says, "Don't you know that your body is a temple of the Holy Spirit who is in you, whom you have from God. You are not your own since you were bought with a price, so glorify God in your body."

Not only is the body called the temple of the Holy Spirit, but it becomes a means by which a Christian is capable of glorifying God. Christ died not just for the Christian's soul, as some seem to think, but also for his body, which was included in the price that He paid. Since the redemption of the body is part of redemption, Paul says, "You're not your own." That means that the body, which God calls His, is now to be used for God to do good. The believer has become a slave of Christ in order to be free to do good. The will of the slave is the will of another. Christian—slave of Christ—God wants to be glorified through your body. All of this is basic to our consideration of the mind-body problem.

Romans 8:11 is an interesting passage because in this verse, Paul is speaking about something that happens to the body right now that he calls a spiritual resurrection of the body:

> *Moreover, if the spirit of the one who raised Jesus from the dead dwells in you, this one who raised Christ from the dead will give life to your mortal bodies through his spirit who dwells within you.*

This is a resurrection of the body to newness of life here. Paul speaks of a new ability—the ability to live for Jesus Christ that the body receives here and now. Romans 12 makes it clear how God has made it possible to present our bodies to God to honor Him.

But the body is also viewed as a problem in the Bible, and it is a problem. Remember the problem that Paul had with his body? Remember how he talks about it in Romans 6 and 7, in particular, how he says that he finds this body hindering him from doing the things that he wants? He finds his body going the wrong direction. All through the New Testament, we read in Paul and Peter, as well as in others, that even this redeemed body has desires of its own that are not always the same as the desires of the Spirit. The body wants to do things; it has its own agenda, you might even say. The body wants to go places and act in certain ways, and respond with certain forms of action. This body, though it has the potential to glorify God, doesn't always, and becomes a problem. Paul seems upset with his body. He calls it a "body of death," and, in near desperation, asks, "Who will free me from this body of death?" He gladly affirms: Jesus Christ will do that. And in the 8th chapter, he talks about how the Spirit of Christ does.

But, clearly, the body becomes a serious problem for the believer. And, if your body isn't a problem for you, then maybe you're not really a believer. Every believer struggles with this problem. Every person who has ever come to faith in Jesus Christ knows that there are things he wants to do for Christ, and yet the body gets in the way. There are things he wants to stop doing that he knows are wrong, and yet the body wants to keep on doing them. That struggle is the whole point of Romans 6 and 7. What's behind the struggle?

The problem is that our bodies have been wrongly programmed by the nature with which we were born. We're born into this world sinners, with a sinful nature that will sin—a nature that was warped and twisted from the day of conception. No child could ever die, no child could ever have a defect, no child could ever be aborted if that child was not considered a sinner, because "the wages of sin is death." And that sin is what has also led to all the distortions and impairments of the body. Thus, from the very beginning, you have a body condemned by God. Every person, body and soul, is condemned by God for his sin. The effects of sin begin to operate from the very earliest moment in a child's life. Because that child, as a sinner, has a corrupt nature, he will go on sinning until such a time as Jesus Christ changes his nature, until the Holy Spirit comes in and regenerates him and gives him a new nature. The new, regenerate person desires and wants to do the things of God. But, during the whole time from the very earliest days on through the whole period before he is regenerated and, perhaps, even for a time afterwards, that sinful nature programs his body. Because its orientation is away from God, it habituates the body so that when adverse things happen (people say something critical, problematic situations develop, pressures come), the body is taught to respond habitually to those circumstances, in sinful ways. This nature programs the body to respond wrongly.

If I had a wand to wave over you, so that you would lose every habit pattern you ever had, so that tomorrow you'd wake up with no habits—none, I mean zilch, zero habits—now, just think what that would be like. You wake up, and there you are with your eyes closed, and you have to think consciously of everything you will comfortably or smoothly do. These are the four characteristics of habit. You can't do anything automatically, unconsciously, comfortably, or smoothly. You're going to be awkward in everything that you do. You're going to feel conspicuous about it; you'll feel uncomfortable.

So, you have to think carefully, "What do I do next? I'd better open my eyes. So, you get them open. Then, you think, "Now, how do I get out of this bed?" You're awkward like a little child who tumbles over the edge of his crib. You have to think, "Do I put the feet out, the hands out, or throw the whole body over at once?" You've got to make a conscious decision about such matters. Nothing is automatic. Nothing is unconscious. Nothing is comfortable. Nothing is smooth. You have no skills. That is, nothing is habitual. Then, you go through all the rituals of putting clothes on. For example, buttoning a shirt. You know now how to button a shirt, but remember when, as a child, you first learned how difficult it was to button something? You don't know whether to begin buttoning at the bottom and go to the top, the top and go to the bottom, or the middle and go both ways. Think about putting toothpaste on your toothbrush. First, you've got to unscrew a cap. You don't have those skills. You finally get it unscrewed, and then you've got to aim it directly at a small, narrow toothbrush. That's hard to do when you have no skills. So, if you get half of it on the brush you're doing well; the other half will go up your arm and wrist. How about getting the brush in your mouth, instead of up a nostril? On and on and on this goes. Why, you would not get to breakfast by midnight!

Almost everything you do involves habit. You live by habit. God gave you a great blessing when he gave you the habit-capacity so you wouldn't have to think consciously about everything you do and go through with the awkwardness of learning to do it as if for the first time, every time. So,

He gave you the skills and the ability to do things comfortably without thinking.

You have the capacity to act by habit, a blessed and wonderful ability from God. This capability, however, may be used for a blessing or a curse. You have learned to respond to life wrongly as a sinner. When somebody says something nasty to you, what is your immediate, your learned, your habitual response? What kind of habitual responses have you built in as a sinner over the years? Do you figure, "I'll get him ten times over?" Do you do good or do evil to those who do evil to you?

Romans 12 says that all sinful habits must change, and you've got to learn to overcome evil with good. That change is not easy, because as a sinner, a little sinner, born a sinner, manifesting yourself as a sinner, right away you began to program to respond sinfully to sinful things done to you. You learned those things so well that you do them unconsciously, automatically, comfortably, and skillfully. Those are the characteristics of habit.

As a Christian, however, you've got to change, and that's the problem that you have with the body. That was the problem Paul had with his body. He wanted to do things God's way, but the body had been programmed to do something else. The lie slipped out before he even realized he'd told it. Then he had to go back and deal with that issue. The nasty word was spoken before he even realized that it was out there. He struggled to relearn and replace those sinful patterns with new biblical ones.

We haven't time to go into that whole dynamic of the "put off" and the "put on" of Ephesians 4 and elsewhere in the Scriptures that talk about replacing habit patterns, but we must at least be aware that this sin-affected body is not the wonderful body that was originally created for Adam. It has become distorted because your soul was passed down corrupted and guilty, and so, it would program the body wrongly. The brain, N.B., is part of the body, and it is the brain that is programmed to see to it that the rest of the body responds sinfully.

At death, you're going to receive a new body, if you are a believer. The new body is going to be like Christ's body. That's what we're told in

Philippians 3:20,21:

> *Our citizenship is in the heavens from which country we await the coming of a saviour, the Lord Jesus Christ, who will transform our degraded bodies, making them conform to His glorious body, by the power that enables Him to subject all things to Himself.*

Though it was created perfect in Adam, this body has been degraded. It was created to glorify God, and did, until the Fall. It was created to be used for His honor, but now the body is used for God's dishonor, as we know. Think of what people do with their bodies, all the horrible things that bodies get involved in, all the wretched things that bodies are achieving in this world against God, rather than for God. The body has been degraded by sin.

But the body of the believer is going to be transformed. It is even being transformed gradually now, but someday that transformation will be perfect. It will possess all the powers, all the new properties that Christ's glorified body now possesses. His body could no longer be subject to pain; it was a body that had powers that we don't even understand. It could pass through the wall of a sepulcher! I'm looking forward to that kind of body. And, I think every physician, in particular, ought to look forward to that kind of body after he or she sees how blighted bodies can become.

So, the body was made good, it became degraded, and now, because of habits held over from his unsaved life, it becomes a problem even to a believer. Someday, however, God is going to redeem the body fully, and Romans 8 talks about that hope in the latter part of the chapter.

I want to stop and consider an implication at this point. Begin to ask yourself the question, "What is the Christian physician's goal in medicine?" The physician deals with the body. Is it your goal to heal? Is it your goal to ease pain? Is it your goal to make life more comfortable? We're not yet ready to answer the question, but we can say this much now: In working with bodies you should certainly be more than a veterinarian. You should show respect for those bodies because those bodies have been made to glorify God. People are more than meat and bones.

Any Christian physician who begins to look on bodies only as bones on which the meat hangs has a very pagan view. What should be your goal in medicine, and what should be your goal in treating the body? Serious questions arise, and we're going to look at some of them as we go along.

The redeemed body is an instrument for service by which a Christian may glorify and honor Christ. In Romans 6, the word "instrument" (also sometimes translated as a "weapon") frequently occurs. "Instrument" or "tool" is the proper translation of *hoplon* in the passage. The *hoplon* was the instrument or the weapon with which the hoplite (Greek foot soldier) fought. It was his instrument, his tool for fighting. In Romans 6 and 7, the *hoplon* was probably some kind of tool that a slave would use, because all the way through this 6th chapter, Paul has been talking about slaves and masters. He talks about sin as the master over us before we come to Christ, so that we are the very slaves of sin.

But, to those who have come to Christ, he says: "Don't present your bodily members to sin as "instruments"—there it is—of unrighteousness, but rather present yourselves to God as persons who have been resurrected from the dead and are living, and your members to God as instruments of righteousness (v. 13)." God wants the bodies of believers as instruments to perform righteousness in this world. Any physician who doesn't have that in the back of his mind as he is working on bodies misunderstands God's purpose for bodies. You must see the body as a tool that God wants used in His service.

Sin was your slave-master. You were born into that slavery to be used by sin. But Christ redeemed and freed you from sin's dominion by the cross so that you could serve Him. Those very same members of your body—hands, feet, eyes, nose, brain—the members or organs of your body that once were instruments for sin, may now become instruments for righteousness. That is a critical point for you to keep in your mind as you think of bodies and what you, as a physician do to them.

And yet, these are broken tools, abused tools, worn tools. The body isn't yet freed from the ravages of sin. It is a living-dying, warped tool, at best. That is what a body is. And, it is interesting that God is willing to use even such tools for His purposes. This requires something of a partnership, an interaction between man and God. We're actually thinking here more of a partnership and interaction than the word "tool" (which speaks almost of something that is inanimate) would imply. This body alone, apart from the spirit, does not constitute a competent person. The body alone is a thing. Yet the brain, which is part of that body, is more than a storage bin. It is an active filing, processing, and controlling agent that distorts, relates, molds, and shapes data that are received according to its own biases, according to its points of view, according to its perspectives and dispositions, as well as according to its physical condition. And, it's that physical condition of the members of the body (which includes the brain) with which you are concerned. As you think of the mind-body problem, you should be concerned about the bodily aspect of this body-mind issue because that is your perspective and your focus.

You, the "you" that people call the "you" and the you that you call yourself, is identified very closely with that body. Your body is acted upon by your mind, and the body itself responds by acting according to its predispositions. There is an interaction within you that makes you, you. At death, the body will be lifeless and mindless. Yet, you will continue to exist consciously when your body is dissolved. You've lost your tool. That's what you can say about death. At death, you will become disassociated from your body: "The body without the Spirit is dead (Jas. 2:26). However, at the present time, the courts rightly consider the body to be you. Right now, police take pictures of the bodily you and hang them on the post office wall. They take this body that they call "you" and put handcuffs on it. They throw it behind bars and lock the doors.

And then, when necessary, they take that body (which they call "you") and execute it in an electric chair. So, now, you are very closely and rightly identified with that body; it is an integral part of the "you" that you are.

But let's now enlarge our previous implication, pausing once again. Your task as a physician certainly brings you to the point where you must deal with sin's effects upon bodies. That is one thing that you are deeply involved in. Since bodies provide man with a means (tools, instrument) for expressing love for God and for one's neighbor, and thus for glorifying God, the highest goal of Christian medicine is not comfort, is not ease, is not healing. The highest goal of medicine is not being patient-centered at all. It is rather to enable a man to use his body to honor God as an instrument of righteousness. That's the goal that a Christian physician should have. But, what if he's an unbeliever, what if he doesn't honor God? That's his, not your problem. You make it possible for him to do so. And if, at such a time as he should be saved, then because of your efforts, he will be in better condition to do so.

Medical help may even speed sanctification (the process of growing out of sin into righteousness) in the sense that it may enable persons to do and think better than they might otherwise. It may even be part of an evangelistic tool so that the person may be enabled to hear and believe the gospel, which he could not do prior to medical help. Therefore, the implication for physicians is that when they repair broken bodies, they are not mere appliance repairmen; they are doing spiritual work. Muse on this point the next time you feel cynicism creeping over you.

I'm sure there are many physicians who get to the place where they see blood and guts enough that it's hard to keep this view of things in mind. I'm sure there are many physicians who begin to work on hunks of flesh and body and bones, sawing them apart, sewing them together, cutting them up, and doing all the things you do to them, who find it hard to remember. But the goal is to enable the patient to honor God in his body. If you are only thinking of healing people, however, and if you are patient-centered, you're going to get discouraged. If you can't see service to God behind what you're doing, and you can't see that you are potentially enabling people both better to hear and to receive the teaching of the Word of God for salvation and for sanctification and to, therefore, fulfill the mandate that God has given to them, then you have missed the major purpose of medical work.

Truly, Christian medical workers see beyond that body to what it can do in the service of Jesus Christ. And, unless you can put Him first, unless your medicine is God-centered, then your work is going to become discouraging, defeating, and grueling, worthless—nothing more.

Mind

Now, when the body, the brain, or some other organ is impaired, the mind is affected, and we'll get to what the mind is in a little while. The body, we said, is like a damaged tool. That means it doesn't function properly. And so, the mind cannot use, or use to the full, that impaired part of that body. Wilder Penfield, the famous Canadian neurosurgeon, who worked for 30 years on brains, treating epilepsy, said that he observed mind acting independently of brain under controlled conditions that were reproducible at will. An interesting book called The Self and Its Brain (the title was changed from The Self and the Brain) by John Echols and Charles Popper, confirmed this view. Both authors are tremendously respected people, with Echols being a Nobel Prize winner and a renowned neurophysiologist. The body, what in you is acted on, by, and in concert with the mind—the body and that mind together—become an acting soul in the service of Jesus Christ. Your spirit uses your body to reach the world. The spirit doesn't directly reach the world. It uses the body to find out through the senses what's going on in this world, and having found out, uses the body as an instrument to do things to and in this world. We need a view of mind and body that begins to orient us in this direction.

In regard to the mind and the body, there are three principal biblical terms:

1. now, the seat of consciousness or understanding, often contrasted with "flesh" as in Romans 7:23,25 and with *dianoia*, a compound word derived from *nous* meaning, "to think or be mindful of;"
2. *phren*, the second of those three words (and the *phren* family words: *phreneo* meaning "to think or be mindful of," and *phren*, meaning basically "midriff," as that was where the thought process was considered to take place by Greeks who invented this word;)
3. *leb*, an Old Testament word (which is also a big New Testament word) for "heart," which covers all the New Testament terms as well. It is the only word in the Old Testament used to refer to the mind, and its use is larger than the mind itself.

The biblical word "heart" needs to be understood, and maybe, we need to take a little while to understand it, because, in Western society, "heart" has come to mean something quite different. When we look at a Valentine, we see little cherry-cheeked cherubs with bows and arrows shooting little arrows into hearts. The meaning of heart in that context (one that comes from the Roman background) in Western society is emotion and feeling. And, when we say, "I love you with all my heart," we are thinking of deep emotions that well up: oceans of emotions. That's not at all what the Bible is talking about when it uses the word "heart."

Whenever you read "heart" in the Bible and think "emotion" or "feeling," you misread your Bible. You have poured new content into the word that the Bible knows nothing about. When a preacher says, "Now, what we need is less head knowledge and more heart knowledge," he is making a totally non-biblical disjunction. Nowhere in the Bible is the head (the intellect) put over against the heart: Cf. "...as a man thinketh in his heart", "The fool hath said in his heart, 'There is no God'" (You know why he's a fool, of course, because he's listening to one when he talks that way). This man is deciding things. Consequently, we read of the "thoughts and intents of the heart" in the Scriptures. So "heart" is not set over against intellect; it includes the intellect.

"Heart" in the Bible, far from meaning emotion, is more often linked with the intellect than it is with the emotions. The word that is used for emotion in the Bible is "gut," "belly." Recall the passages that speak in the Bible about "bowels of compassion." Think of the literal gut feeling you get in an old elevator. You don't feel it in your heart; you feel queasy down in the gut. Biblical writers understood that that's where the feelings, the emotions, were principally experienced. "Heart," then, meant something else.

What does heart mean in the Bible? Well, if it isn't set over against the head, over against what is it set? It is set over against the lips:

> *This people honors me with their lips but their heart is far from me.*

It is set over against the mouth. Romans 10 says,

> *You must not only say with your mouth but you must believe in your heart that God has raised Him from the dead.*

So it is—heart and mouth, heart and lips. In the Psalms we read about the hands as over against the heart. In 1 Samuel 16:7 we read that man looks on the outward appearance but God looks on the heart—the outward appearance as contrasted with the heart. Lips, hands, mouth, and outward appearance are set over against heart. What does "heart" mean? "Heart" means the inner you, the life you live inside of yourself that nobody knows anything else about except God and you. In Acts, when the disciples pray, they pray to God as the "Heart-knower."

When we think of "heart," we ought to be thinking about that inner life of the individual that motivates all that he does and all that he is and all that he thinks. Listen to what Jesus says about the heart in Matthew 15:18:

> *From the heart come evil thoughts, murders, adulteries, sexual sins, thefts, false testimonies, blasphemy.*

This is the source of evil and difficulty in our life. This word "heart," this *phren*—this *leb*, this *kardia*—is also used for "mind" in the Bible, but is bigger than "mind." And, the reason it is used for "mind" in the New Testament as well as these other words for "mind" is because it was the only term they had to use for "mind in the Old Testament. Much Old Testament vocabulary and thought comes over into the New, as well. Remember, Solomon wrote, "keep your heart with all diligence, for out of it are the issues of life." Out of it pour all the streams of your life—every aspect of your life begins, and is motivated by, is centered in, and is initiated by the heart. The heart is critical in Scripture. We must understand it.

What is the relationship between mind, spirit, and soul? At this point, I want to draw a distinction. The real problem is not mind-body. The problem, really, is a spirit-body problem. I don't want to talk so much about a mind-body problem after this, but I want to talk about this spirit-body problem, because, mind is not the only aspect of the problem, and it is part of the larger spirit-body problem.

Matthew 22 is very interesting because of how Jesus quotes Deuteronomy 6:3. He says, "You must love the Lord your God with all your heart, with all your soul, and with all your mind." Jesus added the word "mind." "Mind" was not in the Hebrew passage because, obviously, there was no separate word, as I said, in the Old Testament for mind. "Heart" covered it all. But, Jesus added the word "mind," so that we understand clearly that mind was not excluded in loving God, but that with all that you are, and all that you have, you must love God. John Calvin says that "mind" was added here by Jesus so that "soul" and "heart" would be understood by this new word which had come on the scene in the meanwhile. Jesus didn't want people who had the word "mind" as part of their vocabulary to misunderstand Him. Well, that may be so, but He certainly wants you to know that with all you are and all you have, you are to love God.

The truth is, there are quite a few terms used in the Bible that need to be understood and related to each other. These various terms get their meaning from this mind-body or spirit-body relationship. That's why we encounter various terms like "soul," "spirit," "heart," and "mind." The two terms, spirit and body, for example, stand on their own. The spirit is the immaterial entity that you are, thought of as out of relationship with the body. That is a most important point about its use. For example, in Luke 24:39, Jesus says, "A spirit has not flesh and bones as you see Me have." "Body" means that material entity you are that is not spirit. The interesting thing about "spirit" is that God is called a Spirit in John 4:24. He is never called a soul. And, the Holy Spirit is called the Holy Spirit, and never the Holy Soul. I don't know whether you ever thought of that or not. He is always called the Holy Spirit. The reason for that is because "soul" is the same immaterial you as spirit or 'heart" but in union with and animating the body. The spirit in your body becomes soul. The spirit out of your body is called "spirit." God doesn't have a body so He can't be called "soul" but He can be called "spirit." The Holy Spirit doesn't have a body, so He can't be called Holy Soul, but He can be called Holy Spirit. The spirit, then, is the same entity as the soul, but thought of as out of relationship to the body.

That the immaterial entity, when in relationship with the body, is called "soul," is clear from the creation account. Remember, God breathed into Adam's body, which He had shaped from clay, the breath of life. And, as a result, man became a living soul. So, the spirit or breath is breathed in, and man became an animated being, a living soul. But then James says, when, at death, the soul is severed from the body, the body is dead. The immaterial you (now called spirit) departs from the body, and the body is dead.

"Heart" is also the immaterial "you." It is one and the same with spirit or soul. It is, however, viewed as within you—something that can't be seen or gotten to except by God and, to some extent, by you. "Heart" is your inner self contrasted with the lips, the hands, the outward appearance. It's the immaterial "you" thought of as inner "you," not outer "you," not the "you" that people can see. Not bodily "you," but immaterial "you" in that body. That's what "heart" means. And, "mind," once more, is the same immaterial "you or person self-consciously thinking, willing, remembering, reasoning.

The union of "mind" or spirit with the body forms a functioning unit oriented toward the material world. When the spirit, this immaterial me, is within this body that I also am, then I am oriented towards the material world, spirit, and body. Not to say I don't believe that there is a God and an immaterial world, but I'm not really participating in what goes on in that immaterial world. I am participating almost 100% in what goes on in this world. Though I am in contact with that other world, my present orientation is towards the physical world. This union of body and spirit, rather than called "dichotomy," as some people call it (meaning "to cut into two"), I would rather call "duplexity," (which means two things folded together, two things brought together). Dichotomy speaks of taking the two apart, and we might call that what happens at death (you are dichotomized), but what you are now is a duplex person. The spirit and the body are so united that should we under ordinary circumstances—and I'll explain that exception later—separate the one from the other, you would die, says James.

These two elements, then, are normally inseparable except at death. The only place where "mind" (*nous*) is set over against spirit that I can find is 1 Cor. 14:14-15, where it is talking about praying, not just with the spirit but also with the mind. Probably, he is here saying that the Corinthians thought the human spirit is under the control of the spiritual gifts rather than the gifts under the control of the spirit. That is wrong. What he teaches is that there must be no mindless use of the gifts. That is forbidden in I Cor. 14:32. Yet, that is precisely what many people applaud today. "I put my mind in neutral and let things go." No. He says the mind ought always to be under your control. "The spirits of the prophets are subject to the prophets."

It might be correct to say that the spirit has a mind as the body has a brain. I want to examine that statement a little further, but that's probably an accurate statement. At any rate, this duplexity, functioning in man, this body-spirit thing called "soul," has been scientifically observed, which is unnecessary for faith, but, nevertheless, very interesting. I want to close with some quotations from the work of Penfield and Echols, and some others, just to add that dimension to what we are saying here. Remember, Penfield worked for thirty years cutting the skull cap off and prodding around with electrodes in people's brains observing what happens. In a now-famous paper he says,

> When the neurosurgeon applies an electrode to the motor area of the patient's cerebral cortex, causing the opposite hand to move, and when he asks the patient why he moved the hand, the response is, 'I didn't do it, you made me do it.' It may be said that the patient thinks of himself as having an existence separate from his body.
>
> He explains: "I didn't do it, you made me do it by prodding my body.
>
> Once, when I warned a patient of my intention to stimulate the motor area of the cortex, and challenged him to keep his hand from moving when the electrode was applied, he seized it with the other hand and struggled to hold it still. Thus, one hand, under the control of the right hemisphere, driven by an electrode and the other hand which is controlled through the left hemisphere were caused to struggle against each other. Behind the brain action of one hemisphere was the patient's mind. Behind the action of the other hemisphere was the electrode.
>
> So, we concluded, there are, as you see, many demonstrable mechanisms in the brain. They work for the purposes of the mind automatically when called upon, but, what agency is it that calls upon these mechanisms, choosing one rather than another? Is it another mechanism? Or, is there in the mind something of dif-

ferent essence? To declare that these two are one does not make them so, but it does block the progress of research.

That's part of what Penfield had to say. Let me give you one other comment of his, from another section of his paper that I think you will find interesting. He records one such occasion in which a young South African patient lying on the operating table exclaimed when he realized what was happening, and it was astonishing to him to realize that he was laughing with his cousins on a farm in South Africa, while he was also fully conscious of being in the operating room in Montreal. Penfield observed that the mind of the patient was as independent of the reflex action as was the mind of the surgeon who listened and strove to understand. "Thus," he says, "my argument favors independence of mind action." As Penfield put it, "if we liken the brain to a computer, man has a computer, not is a computer."

This discovery was totally unexpected, but it was in no way singular. It was repeated again and again for hundreds of patients, each of whom could identify the scene recalled with ease, and virtually instantaneously. Patients could elaborate on what they saw and explain the circumstances, much as a TV viewer seeing a serial program might explain the circumstances to a watching companion who was ignorant of the previous events." He's sitting there eating popcorn watching what is going on in his brain, in his mind's eye. "In such a situation there are clearly two elements - the viewer is not part of the TV program but an observer. Yet, he is more than an observer, insofar as the viewer can adjust the set, clarify the image, change the program, and, in recall situations, shut it off at will under normal circumstances by a shifting of attention, that is, tuning into another program.

Here then, we have a dualism of object and subject, of brain and mind. It is no longer safe to view the mind as a computer, though the brain is indeed a computer of extraordinary refinement. But this computer has a programmer, and an operator who is using it as a tool of recall and of motor control. Epileptic subjects may sometimes experience times of total blackout as to consciousness, the mind apparently ceasing entirely to control the brain, providing that the brain has already been programmed, the subject becomes an automaton and completes the task in a state of total mindlessness. Patients may even complete a journey from work by car, provided that the journey is an habitual one, and that no unexpected interference occurs. Navigating the traffic and road turns is done by means of purely conditioned reflexes. Afterwards, nothing whatever of the journey will be recalled. The efficacy of the brain as a computer is, therefore, truly remarkable." Penfield observes that" the continual functions of the normally active mind were apparent in such journeys," but, he emphasized, that" it is the mind that must first program the computer brain since the computer is only a thing, and on its own has no ability to make totally new decisions for which it is not programmed."

"Kornhuber discovered the existence of electrical potentials generated in the cerebral cortex following the exercise of will to action and prior to the actual performance of motor activity. Between the conscious act of will and the activity resulting from it, he consistently observed a measurable interval lasting a few seconds or less. During this brief but highly significant interval there is a flurry of electrical potentials over a wide area that gradually centers or concentrates the signals which then bring about the movement willed. This takes the form of a developing specificity of the pattern impulse discharges until the pyramidal cells in the relevant cortex area are activated to bring about the desired movement. The delay between willing and willed movement is quite measurable. The nature of the will and the resulting willed action correspond. The problem remains, however, as to how the neuronal impulses are set in orderly action by the will. One has to assume," Echols believes, "that there is a bridge of some sort across the interface between the mental world and the physical world. It seems to warn the will is about to act upon the mechanism. No such warning signal or attention-getter seems to be involved when action is involuntary, but consciously willed action takes time to be set in motion. Echols wrote, "I woke up in life, as it were, to find myself existing as an embodied self with this body and brain."

That's the way that he looked at it. As Christians, I think we need to do serious thinking about these matters.

The Biblical Perspective on the Mind-Body Problem Part Two

We come now to the question which is the heart of it all—what is the relationship of spirit to body? Remember, I said that I want to talk about spirit more than about mind because that is where the real issue is. And, we'll see why, I hope, as we observe the relationship of spirit to body in normal activities.

In Gen. 2:7, we read about the creation of man. God first shaped man's body. It was a lifeless lump until He breathed into its nostrils, and man became a living *nephesh* (soul). The spirit that He breathed into man constituted him a living soul. Before that time, the body was mindless. Don't miss that point. Mind was not originally part of the body, but when the body was given life, it began to operate rationally. Mind began functioning; this was man in the fullness of what man is. Man was not truly man prior to that time. Mind entered when life entered, and mind leaves when life leaves. When I look at a corpse lying in a casket, as I did two nights ago, I was not looking at something that possessed mind, because it had no life in it. It was a lump of tissue that once lived but now had lost that dimension. Remember this as we discuss mind (or spirit): that it is not body that is the foundation or source of mind, but the spirit. That activity began only when spirit entered the body and man became a living soul.

These words each have a special meaning. The word "spirit" means the inanimate, non-material part of man viewed as out of relationship to the body; separated from it. That same non-material part of man viewed in union with the body is called "soul." This same immaterial part of man, viewed as the inner you, over against what you and I see and hear—one's outward appearance—is called "heart." The spirit within is called "heart" as over against the body, the lips, the hands, the voice—the outward appearance. That is the way the Bible uses those terms, and it will help to get these straight as you begin to think about them.

The word "mind," then, means a human being functioning in such a way as to remember, think, and decide. At the present time, during the duplex period when body and soul are folded together so that to remove one or the other from that union would bring about death in most instances (and I'll tell you why I'm making that exception later on), you cannot know yourself as pure spirit. Neither can you know yourself as pure body. This fact causes most of the problems that we have when thinking about the mind-body problem.

There is such a close union between body and spirit that we cannot imagine what it will be like to be "unclothed," as Paul called it (2 Cor. 5), when our bodies are laid aside temporarily and we become something less than what man was intended to be (but, this time, in the opposite way). Even though the soul is perfected at death, man is incomplete until a glorified body is someday united to it. But, at this present time, we just can't imagine what that separation will be like. We can only talk about it and understand certain facts about it, but we cannot experience it or even imagine what that experience will be like. Therefore, many of the problems we shall consider can be solved only partially. Some questions must be left hanging. I am not able to answer them because I am neither pure spirit nor pure body.

The members of the body, the *hoploi*, as we saw previously (the instruments or tools that God uses to work through us to understand and affect this material world), include the brain. The brain is to be used by the spirit to serve God, by affecting and being affected by the world. The one exception to which I referred is a most interesting one. It is recorded in the twelfth chapter of 2 Corinthians. Paul here speaks about something that happened to him 14 years before. He describes himself in the third person to avoid boasting. Indeed, the experience was so exceptional that God gave him a thorn in the flesh to keep him from such boasting.

He says, "I shall come next to visions and revelations from the Lord. I know a person in Christ, who fourteen years ago was snatched away to the third heaven." (Incidentally, the Bible doesn't say anything about a seventh heaven. That has to do with movies.) The first heaven is the atmosphere around the earth, as when Scripture speaks of "The birds of the heavens" (or "sky.") The second way in which the word "heaven" is used is of the place where the universe is—the stars, the moon, the sun, the galaxies. The third heaven is where God is. Paul says that he was snatched up to the third heaven. Then he says, in 2 Corinthians 12:2-3:

> *Whether in his body or outside of his body, I don't know, but God does, and, I know this person, whether in his body or outside of his body, I don't know, God knows, was snatched away to Paradise and heard ineffable words that it is not permissible for a human to speak.*

This event raises interesting questions. Paul was postulating the possibility of an OBE (out-of-body experience). He did not say that was how he had experienced these revelations, but he said that was a conceivable way in which it might have happened. He didn't rule it out. He thought one genuine possibility was that, out of the body, he as pure spirit, could, while still living in this world, have had an experience in the third heaven. We'll come back to this later, but that's the exception I have mentioned when I've said that a person cannot be alive when you rip the spirit from the body. James 2:26 says that "the body without the spirit is dead," except, in Paul's very unusual circumstance, we see that such a possibility existed. We'll come back to that in a few moments as we look at some possible implications of Paul's having visited the third heaven without a body in spirit alone. For that matter, the other possibility he mentions, visiting with the body, raises enough interesting issues to keep you busy for the next twenty-five years.

Spirit, or mind, now functions (with this exception) only in the duplex relationship of the body and brain. Duplexity exists to the very end: death. Stephen standing there, being stoned and about to die, says, "Lord Jesus, receive my spirit." He doesn't say,"... receive me," because he is still in that duplex relationship. Yet, he knows that duplexity is about to end. So, he says, "Receive my spirit," knowing that duplexity will soon become dichotomy. He's going to leave that body, and he's going to be received by the Lord Jesus Christ. But, to the very end he still talks about his spirit in his body, because it has yet to be released. It is interesting how one talks about himself. The language used to describe duplexity is informative, especially as the apostle Paul uses it in the sixth and seventh chapters of Romans, where he writes, "I do what I don't want to do, and I don't do what I want to do." Think about the "I" in that sentence!

In 2 Corinthians 4:4 we read that man's mind is "blinded" until such time as regeneration occurs. It's blinded by the sin with which each one comes into this world. Man's corrupt nature keeps him from finding God. Reason cannot take you to God, in spite of some people who think, Thomistically, that it can. The mind itself, is defective. There have been noetic effects of sin upon the capacity to think: that's why we have erasers on pencils. That's why word-processing is so valuable—you don't have to retype everything because of one error. The world's history would have been different had we had computers from the Garden of Eden.

1 Corinthians 2 is a significant passage.

> *When I came to you brothers, I didn't come announcing the revealed secret of God in high-flown speech or wisdom, because I determined to know nothing while I was among you except Jesus Christ and Him crucified. I was with you in weakness and in fear and with much trembling. I didn't deliver my message or preach in persuasive words of wisdom, but with proof and power provided by the Spirit, so that you might not place your faith in human wisdom, but rather in God's power.*
>
> *Of course we do speak wisdom among those who are mature, but it isn't modern wisdom or a wisdom that comes from modern-day leaders, who are coming to nothing. Rather, we speak about God's secret wisdom that has been hidden, that God predestined before time began for our glory. No modern-day leaders have known this; if they had known they wouldn't have crucified the Lord of glory. But as it is written:*
> WHAT THE EYE HASN'T SEEN AND THE EAR HASN'T HEARD, AND WHAT HASN'T BEEN CONCEIVED BY THE HUMAN HEART, IS WHAT GOD HAS PREPARED FOR THOSE WHO LOVE HIM.

> *To us God revealed it by His Spirit. The Spirit searches into everything, even the deep thoughts of God. Who knows the thoughts of a person except the spirit of the person in him. So too no one knows God's thoughts except God's Spirit. Now we haven't received the world's spirit but the Spirit Who is from God, so that we may know that which God has freely given to us. It is these things about which we speak, not in words taught by human wisdom but in those that are taught by the Spirit, combining spiritual teaching with spiritual words.*
> *But a natural person doesn't welcome the teachings of God's Spirit; they are foolishness to him, and he isn't able to know about them because they must be investigated spiritually. But the spiritual person is able to investigate everything while (on the other hand) nobody has the ability to investigate him. WHO HAS KNOWN THE LORD'S MIND? WHO WILL INSTRUCT HIM? But we have the mind of Christ.*

Failure to understand 1 Cor. 2 means inability to understand anything at all about the mind-body problem. Without interpreting the passage in depth, notice that Paul teaches that regeneration is absolutely essential for understanding God's truth. 1 Corinthians 2:14 says that "a natural person does not welcome the teachings of God's Spirit." That means he does not welcome Scriptural teachings. "And, they are foolishness to him, and he is not able to know about them, because they must be investigated spiritually."

Anywhere you are there are sounds and sights that you neither hear nor see. But if you had a television set, you could hear those sounds and see those pictures. The reason that you don't see and hear is because you do not have a receiving set. God says that the unregenerate person (one without the Spirit of God) cannot receive the things of the Spirit of God, because he doesn't have the capacity - the receiving set- to pick them up. Verse 9 says, "As it is written, the eye has not seen and the ear hasn't heard, and what hasn't been conceived by the human heart is what God has prepared for those who love Him." So, the unregenerate human being does not have that capacity, as verse 14 says, to investigate Spirit-given truths, and doesn't welcome them. God has supplied these things only for those who desire them, whose ears have been unplugged, whose eyes have been opened, and whose hearts have been made ready to receive them. In verse 10 Paul writes, "To those who believe in Him, God has revealed these things by His Spirit. The Spirit searches into everything, even the deep thoughts of God." The Holy Spirit is the One who knows the deepest thinking that goes on in God. "Who knows," verse 11 asks, "the thoughts of a person except the spirit of the person in him." Notice, it is the spirit in the person. "So, too, no one knows God's thoughts except God's Spirit." And, then, he says, "Christians have not received the world's spirit, but the Spirit who is from God so that we may know that which God has freely given to us."

In a sense, Paul is saying that when the Holy Spirit enters a believer's life, it is almost like a brain transplant. That's something we can't even fathom or begin to conceive of. We can talk about it with laughter, but the complexities of such a thought far outstrip anything we can ever dream of. But God thought about it. It's like sawing off the top of your skull, removing your brain, and putting God's brain in instead. When the Spirit comes in, the Spirit becomes the receiving set for the things of God. And, so, in verse 16 he says, "we have the mind of Christ" because dwelling within us we have the Spirit who knows the mind of God.

All of the foregoing is to say that the relationship of spirit to body is often thought of in the Scriptures. This question does arise, and the matter does become significant in Scripture; it's not avoided. It's something about which the Bible has a number of things to say, from which we may learn.

Now, we have viewed God's description of the body in normal activity. But, what about bodily injury? What about impairments and incapacities of the body—brain tumors, fevers, comas, drugs, alcohol, various things that affect the body significantly? The question: Is the spirit so tied to the body in this duplex form in which we now live that it loses the ability to relate to this world as the body becomes impaired? The answer is, obviously, "yes." Though the spirit has an interest in doing things in this world, both learning from it by gathering data from it through the senses, and acting toward this world through the members of the body, it becomes difficult for the spirit, when the body is impaired, to do what it wants to do. It has a broken tool that it's trying to use, and finds that this becomes a hindrance. The spirit is hindered from working properly by this damaged tool, and the mind, therefore, does not always function even in full capacity, because, even internally, when a man thinks within himself, as he carries on a dialogue inside, this too depends on the interaction of spirit and body. Even within the mind then, let alone in the outward gathering of data and affecting of the world, bodily impairment causes a problem.

When the body becomes impaired, the spirit does not function with reference to this world as it was intended to. That failure, of course, results from Adam's sin, not necessarily from the individual's sin. The mind functions poorly when it uses inaccurate or inadequate data. If your senses do not work well, then you gather inadequate data. I'm beginning to learn more and more about that. I have a bit of a hearing problem, and people always mumble, it seems. So, through the years, they mumble more and more. It's amazing how they've gotten worse and worse!

If I hear one word and somebody says a different word that sounds like it, I could get a very wrong idea of what he is talking about. My spirit has to operate with the data that it receives through my senses. If it receives inadequate data, then it's going to act in an inadequate or inaccurate way. The reaction may do harm rather than good. Thus the body does affect the spirit in that way. Senility—physical brain deterioration—really is accurately described as losing one's mind, because the mind loses more and more contact with the world when it recedes into the background as brain cells die. The person is not capable of doing things that he once did and is unable to communicate and relate to other people and his world as he previously could. The mind does not function as it should because the spirit is unable to get out there to gather data.

Yet, of course, we know this is not absolute. Even in deep comas, or under anesthesia, the mind may function in spite of the failure of some bodily organ to function. We've all heard of experiences such as, for example, the nurse who was sued because of a comment she made when she thought a patient was unable to hear because of anesthesia. When a fat woman lay on the table before surgery, she said to another nurse, "What is this, another beached whale?" The woman who was anesthetized heard her and sued her afterwards. How much gets through and how much doesn't is extremely interesting.

Then comes the question of death, and the relationship of spirit to body in death. It's from death that we learn a lot about life. It's from this separation of the two that we learn many of the things that we know. That the two aspects of man can be separated and are separated is very plain from the words of Christ Himself. In Matthew 10:28, He says, "Do not be afraid of those who kill the body but cannot kill the soul. Rather, be afraid of the One who can destroy both soul and body, in Gehenna." When He talks about "both" He's making it clear that there are two items, two aspects of man.

Many today will tell you there is no way you can ever separate, even at death, the body from the soul. They simply do not agree with our Lord Jesus Christ. They keep telling us that the Hebrew concept of man did not allow for the separation of one from another. And yet, here is Jesus Christ, with all His Hebrew background, making it explicit that there are two separable elements. Reject that kind of teaching; it will only confuse. This view has been prevalent, not only in liberal circles where it began, but in the last twenty years has gained great acceptance among conservatives who think that man is a unified being, period. On this view, at death, nothing remains. Yet, the opposite is precisely what Jesus was talking about—that the body and the soul can be thought of as separate units, and that they can be treated differently at death as separate units. So, He says "both." Christ viewed man as composed of two elements.

Do I need to turn to Philippians 1:23 for further proof? There Paul says that it is "far better to depart and be with Christ" than to remain in this world. And yet, it was necessary for the Philippians that Paul remain, so that he could be a blessing to them. "Far better" for what? It is certainly not far better for Paul's body for him to depart because the body dies. The body disintegrates. The body rots in the grave. So, he must mean that it is far better for the spirit, which continues after death and is with Christ. He talks about that spirit "departing" and being "with Christ"—literally, "setting sail," as though it were to leave the port behind and set sail for a new adventure. In 2 Corinthians 5:8, Paul describes death as being "absent from the body." Words could not be clearer. To be absent from the body is for the spirit to be "at home with the Lord." What is absent from the body? What is at home with Christ? Certainly not anything material. The spirit is what he refers to. To die, therefore, is "gain," because the spirit leaves this world of sin, sorrow, heartache, and sickness and death behind. It is gain for your spirit to be with the Lord.

The fact that the spirit departs at death raises questions. Stephen can say, "Lord, receive my spirit." Jesus could say in similar language: "Father into Thy hands I commend my spirit." The fact is that he did go into the unseen world. Peter and Acts 2 quote the Psalm that says, "I will not leave his soul in Hades." Don't get the idea that Hades means the place of punishment; it is simply the word that means the "unseen world." The unseen world is composed of both the place of torment and the place of blessing, Paradise. Jesus told the thief on the cross, "Today, you will be with me in Paradise." That's where His spirit went when He died. Nevertheless, it says in the second chapter of Acts that God did not abandon Christ to the grave (Peter is quoting the passage from the Psalm), but He raised that body on the third day. That's the point that he's making.

Now one of the problems related to this concept is that the storage capacity for memory seems to be in the brain. Storage, as Penfield's experiments seem to indicate, is located in various areas of the brain. Stimulate one area and you smell baked goods that you smelled when you were a kid, just as if you were back in the kitchen with mom. Stimulate another chunk of brain and something now appears on the TV screen of your imagination. When people talk about wracking their brains for something they are trying to remember, they express the idea that it is in the brain that memory is stored.

The problem is, then, how does the spirit retain memory after the brain is left behind? That is an interesting question. Does the spirit gain new ways of knowing and remembering? Or, is the brain itself only one way of storing and remembering material? Or, is memory not a capacity that is needed by the spirit in the new world? Does God wipe away all memories of the sinful world from a believer?

But, that doesn't solve the problem because in Luke 16 we have the unbeliever remembering his brothers back on earth. And yet, are we trying to cull too much from that example? Lots of questions arise. I don't have all the answers to them. Note well, however, that mental capacity entered the body as the spirit came in at creation. It seems like the mental capacity that the body possesses leaves when the spirit departs at death. So, in some way, the mental capacity goes with the spirit. I don't understand how it happens, but that is what the Scriptures teach. The spirit is self-conscious (as Philippians says above) when it has departed from the body. As pure spirit, it has been made perfect according to Hebrews 12:23, "... the spirits of justified men made perfect." That, also, is important to understand. The spirit is not perfect in this world and needs to be made perfect at death.

If we were to chart this whole process you could say that at creation, a body and a spirit come together. The spirit brings the mental capacity into being, which becomes a *nousomatic* (mind-body) being. At death, however, when these two separate, the spirit goes to be with God, and the body goes into the ground; mental capacity does not go into the ground but goes with the spirit. The spirit, which was oriented toward this world to work from it and toward it through the body, is now oriented toward the unseen world to work in and toward that world. The laws of working as a pure spirit, in an unseen world, where there is no need for the senses that we depend on today, may require entirely different ways of knowing, remembering, and deciding, which we don't now know about.

Both the spirit and the mind need to be changed in conversion. In Ezekiel 36:26 we read that the Holy Spirit gives a new heart. This heart is this inner you, thinking, willing, remembering. It's the place from which the issues of life flow like streams. That heart, at birth, is a heart of stone, according to Ezekiel, dead as far as the things of God are concerned. It is lifeless, cold, and unreceptive to the things of God. At regeneration, the heart (or spirit) is transformed. It is, says Ezekiel, like ripping out the heart of stone and replacing it with a heart of flesh, that is, a heart that's alive, warm, receptive, malleable, rather than hard, firm, and unmoved. At regeneration, God changes the spirit so that now it seeks and is able to do those things that please God. He enables the spirit to so orient and utilize the body that its members are yielded to righteousness, leading to further righteousness, rather than yielded to sin, leading to unrighteousness. The body, then, is freed from the tyranny of sin, and it is day by day being renewed in its patterns of life. It's being rehabituated just as the spirit within. The Holy Spirit, working through the spirit within, begins to transform one's way of life. These things are all taught in a number of places in Scripture that I haven't time to go into here. But if you want to read further about them, I have considered the question in depth in my book, *Winning the War Within*.

In 1 Peter 1:18, there is a very interesting passage, I want to translate quite closely to the original:

> *Knowing that you were not set free from the useless behavior patterns that were passed down from your forefathers by the payment of a corruptible ransom like silver or gold, but with Christ's valuable blood.*

Christ's blood has set us free from useless behavior patterns that have been passed down through the generations. We are bound no longer by what posterity has said and done and the models they have provided. One tires of hearing people say that you can't love others unless somebody loves you first. They say that you have a wrong view of God unless your father was the right kind of a father, and that models that came out of childhood are so determinative of what we are or what we will become that we are stuck with them for the rest of our lives. That strange dogma is taught even by Christians, though it comes straight out of pagan views of Abraham Maslow. Peter, in contrast, teaches that change is possible. One may break from the influence of the third, fourth, fifth—or hundredth generation. I don't care how many generations have promulgated a way of life; through Christ, a person can break out of that, fully. He is not bound by what his ancestors have done. He is not stuck!

Moreover, it's time to get rid of that Freudianism, which seems to permeate everybody's thinking, and return to the Bible. If the Bible teaches that Christianity does anything, it teaches us that it frees us to serve God—no matter what has happened in the past. It's so tiresome to hear people saying, "I was abused as a child. I've been abused as a teenager." Well, I don't want to minimize the tragedy of true abuse or the sin that was behind it. But, then, psychologists teach people to build a lifestyle around the abuse: "I am an abused person." Not "I'm a farmer, a mother, a child," or anything else. I'm an "abused person." A whole present lifestyle is built around the past.

Do you believe that in Thessalonica and Corinth—where a thousand prostitutes from the temple legally plied their trade on the streets—that in pagan cities of the Greek and Roman world where infanticide was the rule (if the father didn't like the child he just exposed it), do you believe with the kind of background that paganism provided that there was no abuse? Do you believe that nothing wrong was ever done to children, that they all grew up under wonderful, favorable, optimal conditions? Of course not! If anything, things were worse than they are in this country today (as bad as it is here). But, do you ever read, even once, that the apostles Paul, Peter, John, or James said, "Oh, I know you were abused. I know that you have this terrible background. I know all these things have happened to you. You come out of a culture where you've been trained for generations in this way. I don't expect much change from you. I certainly understand and I realize how hard it is to change. I'm not expecting much, or, at least, not much for a long while, until we love you lots so you can learn to love others." Not once do you read that kind of nonsense. What you read is, "You turned from idols to serve the living and the true God." Get with it! That's what you read in your New Testament. You have all the resources in the Word of God and the Spirit of God dwelling within you to do everything that God ever asked you to do. Now, use them! Stop wallowing in the past. The more tragic it may be, the less reason to wallow in it. Romans 5:20 is still in my Bible!

So, then, at conversion, the human being is freed to serve God. That body, which had been held captive and whose members had become slaves of sin, are now freed to become the slaves of Jesus Christ. Rehabituation enables the spirit to function properly toward the world. As one is rehabituated, sanctified more and more, learning to live according to the biblical alternatives and the ways of God, he becomes more efficient in the use of this body not only to evaluate things properly and to store the right kinds of memories - that he can call upon in making decisions in days to come -but also in making decisions right now to do the things that ought to be done. But, the effects of sin on the body—a body that was injured before conversion—if they can be repaired by a physician, will more fully allow for rehabituation and sanctification. Seize that fact brothers! Your job is not merely repairing bodies; it is enabling the spirit to work with and through a body so that God's will can be done, so that the things of God can be accomplished by that body. You, therefore, are involved in a very spiritual activity. I hope you'll remember that when you're just playing around week after week after week with colds and snotty noses and that kind of thing because, even in this, more than a snotty nose is involved.

Now we come to that time toward which everything has been moving in these lectures—some observations, some questions, some answers, and a few conjectures. If my spirit uses my body to gain access to and affect the physical world, through the senses and other bodily members, does physical injury or incapacity (short of death) impair or stop the spirit's learning and functioning? The answer is that it would seem that the body may frustrate the spirit in this as well as in other ways. When the spirit is willing but the flesh (material side) is weak, Paul indicates that problems do arise. Here is a sick person. Here is an old, worn-out body. These people just don't (and are not able to) learn the Word of God well when it is taught to them, or when they study it. Pain may get in the way of study. Dizziness that accompanies atrial fibrillation would certainly do so.

Various kinds of physical problems hinder growth. That means hindering learning as well as functioning in this world. Preachers have to remember this. They can't expect the same results from every person when they teach. But physicians also have to know that they can cooperate with those who are preaching the Word to help wherever they can. You can't make an old body new, and you can't do a lot of things for a body that is incapable of ever going back to an earlier stage, but, where you can, by healing him, you may enable someone to better learn the Word of God, and live more adequately for Christ. Bodily parts, impaired, worn, dulled, or broken, are ineffective tools of the spirit. Therefore, medical efforts that enhance bodily function make greater spiritual activity possible.

Medicine, moreover, may serve an evangelistic dimension, making it possible for some unbeliever to understand the proclamation of the gospel more clearly. The doctor-patient relationship, as a result, is inevitably religious. It is not neutral. It is inevitably a religious relationship because your goal is not merely to heal, comfort, or remove pain, but, first and foremost, to honor God by helping that person to come to faith in Christ. You, as a physician, have a religious relationship to every patient.

It is also true that Christians are obligated to seek medical help. It is true that there is no biblical command to go to a doctor, but the conclusion is inevitable. If we want to be fully capable of doing what God wants us to do, we must do everything we can to bring this body up to snuff so that through it we can serve Jesus Christ as well as possible. That means James 5 must be taken seriously. People have wrong ideas about what is taught in James 5. When James says, if you're sick, you must call the elders of the church, the first thing that implies is that there is an important relationship between Christianity and sickness. It is not that you first necessarily call the doctor, but you certainly do call the elders along with the doctor. In those days, especially in the Roman period, when almost everybody did his own doctoring because there were so few physicians around (and many of them were held in very low repute), the elders did three things: the elders prayed over the patient. (Literally, in the Greek it says "prayed over him.") That pictures somebody in a pretty serious condition so that they must bend over him as he lies on the bed.

The second thing is, if he has committed any sin they probe about it and help him to confess it so that, if this is a judgment of God upon him like those people who were judged for their sin and were sick in Corinth (1 Cor. 11), he would be healed.

But, the third thing that the elders did in a day in which everybody did his own doctoring was to anoint him with oil. People today have made a ceremony out of what was medicine. That passage is not talking about ceremonial anointing at all. The King James did us in again, as it did so many places, by translating two different Greek words by one English word.

There are two words in the Greek that are translated in the King James Version by the English word which means "anoint." Ceremonial anointing—*chreo*—is related to Christos or Christ (the Greek equivalent of the Hebrew *Meshiach*, or "messiah,"), meaning the "anointed one." This is not the word used in James 5. Kings and priests were anointed to set them apart for their work. But that's *chreo*, to pour some kind of oil or water, whatever was used in a given case, upon someone to anoint him, set him aside, to that task. That's not the word that's used in James 5. James' "anointing" is not ceremonial. People go around holding little services in which they take flasks of oil and anoint people. This is totally out to lunch as far as James is concerned.

The word he used is *aleipho*. *Aleipho* is a word used by Hippocrates and all the old Greek physicians. It meant "to rub or smear." It depicts anything but a ceremonial anointing! It was used for rubbing down Greek athletes. Oil and wine, of course, were the two media that were used to rub medicinal herbs into a person's body. That's what James is talking about. Greeks even took oil baths. The elders would administer medicine, just as they would pray, and they would seek to elicit a confession if there was sin involved in this problem. Sin wasn't always involved, but if it was, confession should accompany prayer and medicine. So, at an early date, medicine had a relationship to the person, and he was obligated to do whatever he could do to bring his body into shape so that he could serve Jesus Christ more fully. He was supposed to use medicine, prayer, confess sin—all the possibilities were laid out in James 5.

Now, for a second question or conjecture on the foregoing relationship of spirit and body. If the disembodied human spirit has a mind, that is, it has the capacity to think, reason, and so on (remember mind is not some little organ or a black box; it's a capacity of a human spirit) then this mind must function differently when in a duplex union with the body than when it is not. But that is to be expected since, in the disembodied state, it relates to the unseen world rather than the material world. God is pure Spirit with mental capacity. Mental capacity, therefore, is not tied to the brain. God remembers. In fact, He knows all things from the beginning and all things all the way to the very end. God has total mental capacity, and yet has no physical body. Angels are spirits. They took upon themselves human form now and then and appeared to human beings. But Hebrews says they are spirits sent forth to serve the heirs of salvation. So, here are ministering spirits, angels, who have mental capacity, capability to reason, think, remember, and so on, and yet they don't have bodies, except as they take upon themselves a body to appear in this world to a human being on rare occasions.

When Paul was caught up into the third heaven, he did not know whether this happened in the body or out of the body. The implications of that are several: First, evidently, Paul thought that it was possible to hear, or to see things, and understand things, whatever was revealed to him, as a pure spirit when he was having an out-of-body experience, if indeed that is how it happened. At any rate, he conceived of that as possible. If he didn't conceive of that as possible, he would not have said "whether in the body or out of the body, I don't know." He'd have said, "Well, it had to be in the body because that couldn't happen out of the body." But, as it is, he assumed it could happen out of the body. That is, as a spirit, he could have engaged in mental activity that did not require the use of his body. Certainly, Paul thought it possible under extraordinary circumstances for a body to continue to survive without the spirit. Seemingly contrary to James 2:26, which must have been the general rule, Paul contemplated an extraordinary circumstance. Here was a body still surviving on earth while the spirit had left it. Then, the spirit returned and the body's soul continued in duplexity. Now, was Paul's body dead—that's the only other possibility—in some sense during that period, or was there some kind of a coma, some kind of a circumstance, where the spirit left and the body became mindless? Did the spirit enter heaven for a time while out of that body, and yet that body survived?

If so, some very interesting things are possible. Can it be that a body sustained on life-supporting systems may be kept alive as a corpse full of tissue that's alive (like tissue can be kept alive in a petri dish) while the spirit has already left and gone to be with God? Is that possible? Was that little baby in that condition this past week when her doctor, after six codes, still was trying to keep the baby alive, and I was gritting my teeth more and more and more. He was giving her family false hope. I don't know the answer to that, but I can conceive of that as a possibility that perhaps, in some situations where "heroic" measures are used, we have already had death, that is, the separation of the spirit from the body, and all you're doing is retaining some tissue. Now, I know there are tremendous implications, if that could ever be proven true, such as implications about harvesting organs, etc. But, I'm just asking the question, and it does pose itself, if you think about this situation.

In Revelation 1:10 and 4:1,2, we read that John was "in the spirit" on the Lord's day. And, as such, he went and saw revelations of various sorts and heard various things. All throughout the book of Revelation it said, "Then I saw ..." "Then I heard..." "Then I saw ..." "Then I heard ...." It seems that John had the same sort of experience as Paul (or at least Paul contemplated). John definitely seems to have had an OBE. The spirit alone was hearing and seeing, conducting activity, mental activity. Paul considered that spirit alone might engage in mental activity, even though it was brainless activity, toward the non-material, unseen world. And the body was probably not dead. In these unusual circumstances, that means the spirit can act toward the unseen world now. If Paul went to Paradise in the body, then other problems arise. Was he somehow enabled to see and hear that which a physical being cannot ordinarily see or hear in the invisible world? An interesting question! The question arises in the Old Testament passage, 2 Kings 6:16, 17, where Elisha says, "Those who are with us are greater than those who are against us," and suddenly all heaven was full of chariots and armies that could not be seen normally but were seen in that extraordinary circumstance. So there are many things about this invisible world, and the visible world in which we live, that we don't know much about.

But the problems with the spirit are the same as those we have with heaven and hell, and with the unseen world in other respects. We have to use language and images from this world to describe something very different. Therefore, our descriptions are neither detailed nor final. They only give us some indications of what these things are like. And, often, language can be no better than negative when we talk about the invisible world, i.e., the not-visible world. We don't use a positive word to tell us what invisibility means. When we talk about God being "infinite," we mean He is not finite, but we don't know what we are really talking about beyond that. And, if we talk about heaven being paved with streets of gold, these are the best images we can find for something that is far more wonderful. We talk about hell being like a lake of fire, where the smoke of their torment ascends up forever and ever. Probably hell is far worse. Yet, that is the best human description we can get of it. We're limited considerably when we talk about these things.

Even in this world, some sort of distinction may normally be recognized. For instance, the biblical outer-inner distinction is continually made about people who are here now, as though we can recognize that distinction. We read about the hands, the lips, the mouth, the outward appearance over against the "heart." In 2 Cor. 4:16 Paul thinks that way about himself. He says, "As a result, we don't give up even though our outer person is decaying because on the other hand, our inner person is being renewed daily." Paul is saying, "I'm coming apart at the seams physically. The outer man, the physical being, the body that I have is decaying. It's going to pieces. Yet, this inner person that I am, this non-physical part, is being renewed daily." Now, Paul couldn't have spoken of a physical renewal because it was the body that was physically decaying. Physical strength is precisely what he was losing. So, this renewal must involve strength of purpose, resolve, etc., that came from the Scriptures, as the Spirit of God ministered those things to him.

In 1 Cor. 2:10,11 Paul says that the Holy Spirit knows the deep things of God, and that He knows them just as a person's spirit knows his own thoughts. Notice, he doesn't say brain, or just that the person knows, but that the spirit knows. He locates knowledge in the spirit. He is using the relationship of man's spirit and body to show the relationship of the Holy Spirit to God. The spirit is identified in that passage with mind. When we receive the Holy Spirit, we receive the mind of Christ. That is to say, we can think as God does, think His thoughts after Him. Remember Isaiah 55:8, which says, "Your ways are not My ways, your thoughts are not My thoughts." What does God do? Change His ways and change His thoughts? No. God demands that we change our ways and thoughts so that we begin to think His thoughts and walk His ways after Him. In Hebrews 4:12 we read that God's Word judges the desires and the thoughts of the heart. It gets down to the very innermost part of our being.

Now, consider the question of demon control, which I am not going to get into in any depth. Demonic control of men seems to indicate something about the body being used by a spirit. In this case, it is a spirit other than the spirit of the individual. The spirit of the demon is in control of his body, using it to do things—destructive things, evil things. The demon used that body as a means of getting at the world. In this case, the control and thinking come from a person other than one's self. How does the spirit enter? Does the demon control the person's spirit entirely? Partially? Does it get in between, so to speak, the spirit of the individual and the body, interposing itself in some way? Does it take the human spirit captive and use it in some way to control the body? We don't know. But, in some way, it stands in the position of that human spirit. Possessed persons are used, just as our bodies are "possessed" by our spirits to be used for God's honor.

When one is "absent from the body," at rest, and "present with the Lord," selfhood or "I-ness" passes exclusively to the spirit. We don't read that I am in the grave and I am in a place where I am with the Lord. There is no split in the personality. I am with the Lord. Selfhood goes along with the spirit, and the body is no longer the self. It is no longer "I." People may become preoccupied with a body, but the body is no longer that person. That person has gone, set sail, left the harbor behind. It's possible to amputate large sections of the body and/or replace large portions with transplants or prostheses. Yet, the individual remains the same person.

I suppose it's theoretically possible over the years to come, to replace almost every part of one's body, so that a person is only 10% of whatever he was when he first came on the scene. Now, he is all plastic and tubes, or contains pieces (transplants) from other individuals, or a combination thereof, or whatever, and yet he is still the same person; he has the same social security number, you might say. And, he would be the same "social security number" before God, even if he were not, before men. I won't even try to think about what a brain transplant might mean should that ever be possible; we can't even conceive of it now. But, I would think that, if it were possible, a transplanted brain relating to a spirit in a body into which it was placed could not be another person if the spirit remained, because the spirit/mind continues when the body is buried at death, and that new brain would be buried at death as well. Of course, the spirit would have to deal with a whole new set of stored data, habituations, etc. It is almost unthinkable. But, thinking of it gives you the concept that the continuation of the person, of the selfhood, of the "I-ness," is with the spirit, not fundamentally with the body. Does duplexity make the possibility of such transplants always, forever impossible? I would think, probably, so. Last of all, among these observations, weird thoughts, and so on, consider truth-telling by physicians. Patients have a right to know what the doctor knows about their condition. Under many circumstances, to withhold this is pure theft. However, the issue in many cases may not be whether to tell someone, but when. The doctor may have to wait until the spirit has full enough bodily access to the data to understand and make intelligent decisions. When a person is feverish, when a person is only half with it physically, and his spirit is not operating through that body efficiently, a person may misunderstand a great deal of what you say. Thus, there are times, I would think, when it isn't wise to tell the whole truth and nothing but the truth because the person can't receive the whole truth.

All in all, the mind (spirit)-body problem is both perplexing and fascinating. I have only scratched the surface today. Go on thinking and contributing to this issue. After all, only Christians can think properly about the matter because only they begin from a foundation of God's Revelation.

Biblical Counseling and Practical Calvinism[1]

It is my privilege and pleasure to participate in producing this Festschrift in honor of Dr. Clair Davis. Clair, a good friend, would be happy with the topic given to me: 'Biblical Counseling and Practical Calvinism'. Clair always had more of a leaning to the practical than most of the other faculty I have known.

My title, 'Biblical Counseling and Practical Calvinism,' means that counseling must be Calvinistic to be biblical and practical. I heartily affirm both of those claims. There are, of course, those who would dispute that statement. I shall not argue the case for practical Calvinism being biblical in this place,[2] but shall merely attempt to demonstrate the fact.

Biblical Counseling is Calvinistic

The fundamental principle of Calvinism is that God is sovereign. The fundamental principle of biblical counseling is that God, not the counselor, changes people in ways that please Him. The two principles mesh much better than a hand in a glove. All else in the Calvinistic system grows out of the fact that God *is* sovereign. Few Christians of any stripe, when pressed, will dispute God's sovereignty. Yet, when it comes down to it, only the Calvinist defines sovereignty in a way that preserves it. Others make man more than he is and God less than He is.

---

1 This essay was first published in Peter A. Lillback, ed., The Practical Calvinist: An Introduction to the Presbyterian and Reformed Heritage (Fearn, Ross-shire, UK: Christian Focus Publications, 2002).
2 In my view, Calvinism is simply biblical Christianity spelled out in systematic form.

In Calvinistic thought, sovereignty means that from all eternity God decreed everything that ever has or will come to pass. This biblical doctrine is expressly taught in Ephesians 1:11 where we read,

> *In Him we were chosen as His inheritance, being predestined according to the purpose of the One Who is operating everything in agreement with the counsel of His will.*

In this statement it is also clear that God providentially works in History to bring about His purposes without any flaws or glitches.[3] To be able to plan all things and see to it that all things happen according to that plan is sovereignty.

The sovereignty of God is the basis for Christian counseling. If we could never be sure of God's promises because He is learning and reacting to man—as process theology (recently revived) teaches—we would have no reason to expect that the counsel that we give will hold true. It could change tomorrow with the One Who may have changed His mind today. In fact, counseling might not even need to be biblical, since the Bible would run the risk of becoming outmoded by new, innovative thinking on God's part!

Christian counselees who ask, 'Why did this have to happen to me?' (one of the questions most frequently asked of counselors) need a rock-solid answer. They need to know that, no matter how serious the problem that led to the question, God is in absolute control. It is because Romans 8:28 is the promise of the sovereign God, Who does not change His mind, that Christians have been known to bear up under the most trying circumstances. That is practical Calvinism.

While through tears and pain the believer may have difficulty seeing *how* the promise is true, he can at least understand that somehow trials 'work together' to make him more like Christ (*cf.* Rom. 8:29). And he can begin to bring his faith to bear in the trial to see that this end is achieved. God plans all things for His glory and the believer's good. That is the assurance that sovereignty lends to counseling.

---

3   N.B., He is now '*operating* everything *in agreement with* the counsel of His will'. What He wills to come to pass, he works to bring to pass!

A counselor who doubts that God is sovereignly bringing about all events (including tragedies) for the good of those who love Him, will be stumped by the question. He is likely, therefore, to revert to mysticism, agnosticism, or the like: 'It will all come out well, somehow,' or 'No one knows how there can be evil in a good God's world.'[4] But such responses are worse than unhelpful—they only confuse and engender more doubt. On the contrary, Calvinistic counselors will firmly affirm that God is in charge and that in His time and way, He will work *even this* out for His honor and the counselee's blessing.

Because God's sovereignty extends to *everything* (Eph. 1:11), it extends to salvation. The facts that the famous 'Five Points of Calvinism' systematize bear significantly upon counseling. While there is not ample space to develop the relationship between those facts and counseling adequately, I should like to mention at least a few ways in which this is so.

Take the fact of total depravity.[5] What teaching could be more practical in counseling? Adam's sin plunged us all (Christ excepted) into guilt and corruption. The former is dealt with by God's act of justification, the latter by His act of regeneration, which makes sanctification possible. Sanctification is gradual, halting, spotty, and irregular. Clair, in his inimitable way, once illustrated the process of sanctification by saying that if you wished to graph it, it would look like someone playing with a yo-yo while ascending a flight of stairs.

Biblical Counseling is Practical

Of what practical value are these truths to the biblical counselor? Since every aspect of man has been affected by sin, there are noetic effects of sin in all of us. Man errs, makes wrong decisions, and views life from a distorted perspective. God once put it this way, 'My thoughts are not your thoughts, neither are your ways My ways' (Isa. 55:8, Berkeley). When he attempts to correct his wrong ways by wrong thinking, the ways he adopts lead him into more and more unrighteousness, a phenomenon that is well known to all biblical counselors.

---

4 For more on this see my book, *The Grand Demonstration*.
5 Total depravity means man is corrupt in all his parts; not that he is as bad as he might be.

Those who believe that there is some aspect of man to which they may appeal will tend to address his problems by offering human wisdom and even recommend counseling by unbelieving practitioners. They know, as Paul taught Galatians 6:1, that believers should be 'restored' only by 'those who have the Spirit'. Truly Christian counselors are biblical precisely because they know that it takes the Spirit working using His Word to replace 'depraved' thinking with godly thinking that will lead to godly ways. Likewise, they refuse to incorporate the theories of depraved men into their counseling practice.

Because 'biblical' counselors believe in progressive sanctification, they reject those all-at-once plans of escalating to a 'higher plane' by following some man-made recipe. They know that the 'flesh' must be put off gradually as it is replaced by biblical alternatives. They will settle for nothing less than change that God's Spirit produces, knowing that all other change is useless.[6] They view counseling not as some important thing in itself, but consider it an aspect of the sanctification process. When the process of sanctification is impeded by a log jam, the counselor's task is to break the log jam so that the process may continue unabated. Remedial counseling, therefore, is largely an emergency measure. This eminently practical view of counseling grows out of the Calvinistic interpretation of the Scriptures.

Because they believe that man has been affected adversely in all aspects of his being, biblical counselors work closely with physicians, recognizing that the inner spiritual side of man (variously styled 'heart, spirit, or soul') and the outer physical (body or flesh) interact and influence one another.

Unconditional election is a truth that strikes at the heart of man's problem with sin. When Adam sinned, it was in response to an appeal to become like God. Pride and sinful ambition certainly were involved at the core of his rebellion. Ever since, biblical counselors have had to deal with pride. It lies in the background of nearly every counseling difficulty.

---

6 They will knowingly counsel no one but believers. God has not called counselors to move people from one lifestyle that is displeasing to God to another that is equally displeasing to Him (cf. Romans 8:8: 'Those who are in the flesh *cannot* please God' [emphasis mine]). Until converted, unbelievers cannot think or do those things that God requires. Therefore, biblical counselors evangelize unbelievers rather than counseling them.

The fact of unconditional election stands over against human pride. When God elected Israel as a nation, He drove home the unconditional nature of His choice:

> *It was not because you were greater in numbers than any other nation that the Lord fastened His affection upon you and chose you; for you were the least of all peoples. No, it was because the Lord loved you and on account of His oath which He had sworn to your fathers ...' (Deut. 7:7, 8a).*

And the oath, and that covenant to which it belonged, were also unconditional. God did not choose the fathers because of anything exceptional in them, but out of His own sovereign plan and purposes. The same is true of all those elected to salvation today (Rom. 9:11-13).[7] God's own sovereign choice flows from Him alone and is dependent upon nothing else (Eph. 1:4, 5, 11). Indeed, everything within us would seem to have militated against the choice. Paul says that it was 'when we were weak ... while we were still sinners ... while we were enemies' that Christ died for us, the ungodly, who are now reconciled by His death (Rom. 5:6, 8, 10).

Pride, as Proverbs 13:10; 16:18 warns, lies somewhere behind all 'strife' and 'goes before destruction'. Husbands and wives, business associates, and members of the same congregation contend with one another out of pride, as every biblical counselor knows. He will search it out and meet it with the Calvinistic teaching of the unconditional election of God's own. Instead, he will seek to foster humility that accords with God's dictum in 1 Peter 5:5, knowing that 'God opposes the proud but helps the humble'. He will not be swayed by the faddish views of those who promote self-esteem teaching. He knows that such humanistic teaching results only in greater pride and selfishness.[8] Rather, he will help counselees to make a sober evaluation of themselves, stressing that they must 'not think more highly' of themselves than they ought to (Rom. 12:3). After all, they were chosen not because

---

7 See *The Grand Demonstration* for an exposition of Romans 9.
8 [8] See my book, *The Biblical View of Self-esteem, Self-love and Self-Image.*

they were more lovely, more loving or more lovable than others, but solely because of the grace and mercy of God. Beliefs other than Calvinistic ones tend to minimize the grace of God at some point or other and tend to maximize human initiative.

Due to divorces, the death of a spouse, and other factors, many counselees are lonely. They find it difficult to make new friends. They long for companionship. The truth of limited atonement, properly ministered by a caring counselor, can meet that need as no other doctrine can. It teaches that not only did Christ's death satisfy the Father, but, by His appeasing sacrifice, the Father demonstrated His electing love for individuals. There is One Who loved them *individually* from all eternity. Jesus did not die for some faceless abstraction like 'mankind'. The believer, with all truth, may say, 'He died for *me*.'[9] Luther, more a Calvinist than many present-day Lutherans at this point, commenting on verse one of the twenty-third Psalm once said, 'Thank God for personal pronouns!' In his loneliness at the castle, he could find fellowship with the One Who died for him.[10] The believer knows that 'there is One Who sticks closer than a brother' (Prov. 18:24), and that He will never leave him or forsake him (Heb. 13:5). It is this marvelous truth that Calvinistic counselors have at their fingertips, ever ready to use to comfort and cheer lonely counselees.

Because there are those who think that they have to come to the Father in their own strength and power, but who fear they do not have the power to do so, the truth of irresistible grace helps immeasurably. Jesus said, 'When I am lifted up from the earth, I will draw all sorts of people to Myself' (John 12:32). They do not come on their own initiative; He draws them. They have no initiative until He, by His Spirit, gives them initiative. There is no excuse for lingering when the gospel call goes forth, like so many in Puritanism did, 'preparing' and waiting for some special 'sensibility' that the Spirit was at work. On the contrary, they ought to reach out with the hand of faith and receive the great salvation that was wrought for them. The very desire for it and the will to believe are themselves given to the elect by the Spirit, Who makes them anxious to

---

9   Cf. Galatians 2:20.
10   Cf. 1 John 1:5-7.

be drawn, ready and able to believe.

That at no point does our salvation depend on us is a cheering doctrine, the principles of which extend to all the requirements for living a life pleasing to God. Anything good in us, anything worthwhile that we achieve, is due to the grace of God working in us. Listen to this great counseling passage: 'It is God Who is producing in you both the willingness and the ability to please Him' (Phil. 2:13). *You* do it, but by His wisdom and strength, not by yours! You *pursue* the fruit of the Spirit, but when it grows, you must call it *His* fruit.[11] From beginning to end, all that a believer achieves is the result of the gracious work of the Spirit Who dwells within and energizes him to do good works. This is most encouraging to counselees who recognize their own sin and their utter inability to accomplish what they want to accomplish in their own strength.

Finally, the teaching that it is by God's grace that saints persevere in believing and, therefore, can never be lost, is truly comforting. This is especially true for those who, apart from this biblical understanding, would spend much of their lives focusing on themselves and their future destiny, often doing so in agony, as some do who disbelieve this doctrine. The most astute of those who think that Christians may apostatize and overthrow their faith, after trying in vain to 'keep themselves in the faith' soon recognize the impossibility of attempting to do this and give up, often in despair, abandoning themselves to godless living and its consequences.

The Calvinistic counselor takes his counselee to 1 Peter 1:3-5 where he reads about the 'living hope'[12] God provides for His own. What is it? Listen to Peter when he describes that hope. He tells the Christian that it is

> *an incorruptible, unspotted and unfading inheritance that has been kept in the heavens for you who are guarded by God's power through faith that is ready to be revealed in the last time.*

---

11 See my book, *A Theology of Christian Counseling*, p. 250 ff. for a full discussion of this matter.
12 Hope, in the Bible, means 'confident expectation' of something that God has promised and, therefore, is certain. It is not the hope-so 'hope' that we use the word 'hope' to express today.

Carefully examined, among other things, these verses teach that
1. nothing can go wrong with the inheritance and
2. nothing can go wrong with the heir.

Thus the hope is assured. How useful this, and many other passages that teach the perseverance of the saints are! One wonders how any counselor may counsel effectively who does not believe this biblical teaching.

So, from this very brief glimpse at how Calvinistic teaching is both biblical and practical in pursuing the work of Christian counseling, you can begin to see that when it is set forth only abstractly, Calvinism may seem dry and sterile, as many have charged. But it was never intended to be represented that way. The system must be applied in all of its richness and wonder to struggling saints from the pulpit, in the counseling room, and by the fireside in the home. Then, and then alone, does it come alive, throbbing with life. Then, and then alone, in all of its flaming brilliance it warms the hearts of those who properly understand it. Calvin's symbol of the faith as a flame in the hand says it all.

Design for a Theological Seminary[1]

Today it is almost axiomatic for laymen and pastors alike (less frequently, this is even heard among theological educators) to criticize theological seminaries for the inferior product that they turn out—and there is good reason for doing so. There have been far too many poor preachers, inept counselors, mediocre leaders, etc., pouring forth from the halls of our seminaries. Many of you who read these words know how frightfully ill-equipped you were when you graduated. No wonder there are so many wrecks along the way—lives of would-be ministers, shattered on the doorsteps of first or second pastorates, and congregations split three different ways! Clearly, it is time for a change! By making your concern known to your alma mater or your denominational school, you—as a pastor—can make an impact that (perhaps, in time) will bring about the needed change. That is why, in the sketch that follows, I have suggested some concepts you may wish to explore with those seminary officials upon whom you might have some influence.

How shall the change be effected? Where shall we begin? Shall we bulldoze everything in sight; shall we merely make a few additions to and alterations of the status quo? Neither approach will do. What is needed is radical, basic change, largely within the present framework (loosened up to accommodate it). The suggested proposal that follows has a number of points that cover the whole territory, but it holds together as a complete program. The details must be left to those who actually affect it.

---

1 * Reprinted from *Journal of Pastoral Practice* 3, 2 (1979).

VISION

Those who found a seminary, or who radically change its course, must be men of vision. They cannot think narrowly or negatively. If they do not see clearly where to go, they should not begin the journey. Far too often, evangelicals have shown a great lack of vision.

Vision in goals and programs (to be discussed later) is absolutely necessary. But, here I first mention one thing of lesser importance, though not unessential. Because it is concrete, it often shows the way the wind is blowing, the sort of support one is likely to receive, and the commitment (or lack of it) that a board actually has. I am thinking of the sort of property, building program, and provisions made for the seminary and its programs. Boards must not think merely of the present (or even near future); they must be far-reaching in their outlook.

A seminary needs an expansive outlook. Not only ought it to expect to train future leaders of Christ's church, but a seminary with a truly adequate program will attract many men already pastoring churches for a large variety of continuing education programs. There will be many opportunities for instructing laymen, especially elders and deacons. Conferences of various sorts will be held. The seminary grounds will provide the physical location for any number of special meetings; indeed, a seminary—for the sake of the students and faculty as well as others—ought to be a constant beehive of Christian activity, study, and thought, a focal (and rallying) point for Christian programs. Grounds and facilities designed for such purposes ought to be conceived from the outset of any new concern for seminary education. If such events are worth taking place—if it is proper to give time and thought to them—the seminary should promote them and thereby bring its students into contact with them—right on its own grounds. A vital mix of classroom and ministry must be maintained at all times. Not only will bringing pastors back onto the campus for continuing education and sprinkling them freely into classes with undergraduates help to achieve this mix, but also providing a large variety of meetings and activities such as I have just described.

Students must be challenged continually with the application of truth to life and ministry. Otherwise, they will tend to become cold, bookish, academic, and boring in their approach to God's Word. *Above all else*, everything possible must be done to avoid this, while encouraging a warm, vital, life-changing, committed outlook instead. Cramped thinking—coupled with dusty study—accounts for much of the failure of modern seminary education. Vision—even in the design and purpose of seminary facilities—can do much to offset such dangers (more basic solutions to the problem follow). Narrow, stingy thinking about the physical plant is a clear indication of a board's lack of vision.

PROGRAM

Over the years, conventional seminary training has exhibited both excellencies and failures (so far I have spoken only of the latter—let me here emphasize the fact that there are many good things that *must not* be abandoned). While retaining (for instance) the high level of scholarship that most seminaries seek to achieve, and the clear doctrinal stance that one associates with a seminary to which he adheres doctrinally, changes must be made. It is a mistake to think that the alteration of method and goal in a program designed to bring about a better finished product must necessarily weaken scholarship or doctrinal emphasis. It may, of course, but if the program consists of a more fruitful outworking of what that scholarship has unfolded and what that doctrine points to (and now yearns for), changes for ill need not be feared. Mostly, objections to change come from (1) those who see an unbiblical disjunction between scholarship/doctrine and life/ministry, or (2) perhaps more frequently, those stodgy professors who don't care to be unsettled from their comfortable perches in theological halls, where they can chirp endlessly about the most esoteric aspects of biblical study which happen to interest them, but which provide little help for budding young pastors who will probably never use such "truth" in their ministry. This happens when professors themselves become detached from the ministry of the Word. The model of a seminary (and seminary program) that follows deals summarily with this problem.

How shall we begin to improve upon the program that we have at present, radically changing it, while retaining its excellencies?

First, I propose to *add* a fourth year of training, plus three years of update and advice, and new goals, together with a fresh approach to teaching and curriculum.

I expect to explain these proposals in sequence. N. B., however, I cannot spell out all the details—these would (necessarily) differ from place to place anyway. Indeed, a proper sort of faculty, gathered together with the leadership, should enjoy doing just that. Right now, then, I can offer but a *sketch*.

FOURTH YEAR

The first change that I suggest is a significant one. Let's contemplate it for a time. This fourth year will not be added to the end of the present three; nor will it interrupt them (as the so-called "clinical year" does). Rather—and this is the new feature—it will occur at the outset. This will be a required pre-seminary year prior to taking residential work at the seminary itself.

This year will be spent in a local church. In that pre-selected congregation, the potential seminary student will follow a prescribed program designed by the seminary and supervised by pastors and elders who have been trained by the seminary to do so.

During the year, the prospective student will test his gifts, be exposed to all aspects of the pastoral ministry (including many of the problems involved in it), will be carefully evaluated by the church, will study the elements of Greek by remote learning, will do a good bit of basic reading, study English Bible, and (the hope is) will grow in many ways that will truly prepare him for the three-year seminary program.

What are some of the reasons for this pre-seminary year? Let me suggest just a few (there are many others).

One fundamental reason is to break up the academic syndrome found in so many students, whereby they find it possible to proceed from kindergarten through graduate seminary training without stepping outside a classroom into the rain. They have no practical experience whatsoever, know little about working with people, think of pastoral work only from a theoretical viewpoint, and don't even know how to ask practical questions.

This year is structured to screen out—and to screen *in*—students. Some, who do not belong in theological seminary (and, even theological educators will tell you there is an abundance of these), will never make it; others, who are not yet ready to be thrown immediately into the seminary context, will be better prepared as the result of spending this time in a warmer, more personalized context. These days, there are many conversions taking place during college years, especially (it seems) during the senior year. These students often think they are called to the ministry, but have had no time to *test* their gifts. Some are called, some are not. Those who are not will profit from the year and be directed into another course. Those who are, but who have little acquaintance with the pastoral ministry, will gain much. Men who have been converted long before, who are quite familiar with the ministry, etc., can profit by beginning to develop skills and facing new problems in a more intensive ministry.

The acclimatization of foreign students (always a problem for the seminary as well as for the student) for a year in a congregation will be a very positive factor. They can learn about the American church scene, become better acquainted with the English language, and (in general) become assimilated into the American culture in a loving way. Interested church members can be of great benefit to them while (themselves) being blessed for their loving concern.

And, of course, that year will provide more *time* for training. Moreover, the student will come to the seminary with a notebook full of practical questions in all areas of pastoral ministry (prescribed, reviewed, and approved for admission) that he wants answered during his seminary training (before graduating from the seminary, these answers again will be reviewed and approved). His own inadequacies in ministry will be more apparent to him, as well as his strengths, so that he will be more sensitive to those areas where he needs to concentrate his efforts to acquire the requisite information and skills to become a competent minister.

But of first importance, the pre-seminary year will allow the church to tell the seminary who is fit to be trained for the ministry of the Word—rather than the other way around. For too long the shoe has been on the wrong foot. This fact will place the responsibility where it belongs—upon Christ's church. The church can better evaluate a man's gifts, attitudes, abilities, and commitment because of its peculiar context. The church, ideally, should be willing to put enough confidence in a man to elect him to an office in the congregation during that year. Ideally, only ordained men bearing the church's official approval should enter seminary.

The pre-seminary year will fit into an overall program in any number of ways—there should be flexibility built in—but one basic format looks like this:

Pre-seminary year	—	September to June
August	—	elements of Hebrew at the seminary
September on	—	three years at the seminary

In this way, both the elements of Greek (done during the pre-seminary year) and the elements of Hebrew will be out of the way *before* the student begins his three years of seminary training. This allows the use of the languages in all courses *from the beginning*, and keeps those language courses from vying with other studies (as they so frequently do now). In the long run, better language training is possible.

Following the three years in resident seminary training, there will be three more years of updating and advice.

THREE POST-SEMINARY YEARS

What is this update and advice? And what is involved in postgraduate training? Basically two things.

During the three years following graduation, each graduate will receive two free weeks of updates each year—that is, information about new facts, data, discoveries, studies by faculty members, new trends in the Christian world, etc. This will update students, but it will also tend to keep faculty members in touch with the practical concerns of pastors.

And, perhaps of greater significance, the graduate will be given personal advice on his pastoral ministry. During those first three years, more congregations are destroyed and more young pastors are lost to the ministry than at any other time. This addition will be an attempt to conserve men and preserve churches. Just think what it would have been like for you to have been able to do this, pastor!

The first three years (six weeks in all) would be tuition-free to graduates (a limited number of others may come for a fee), and graduates may continue to come thereafter for a fee. This yearly two-week period of update and advice might be included in a January winterim sandwiched between two semesters. This, too, might be a good time to train pastors as supervisors for the pre-seminary year. Other activities fit this slot nicely, too.

GOALS

New goals must be set for the three-year residential program at the seminary. Two dimensions must be added to the current focus of the seminary. Presently, the emphasis of the typical seminary is upon knowledge—its dissemination and acquisition. This emphasis on knowledge *must not be diminished*. Basically, all the knowledge now taught (though esoteric specialties of certain professors, overlap in courses, etc., should be eliminated) in a good seminary should be taught as it has been (though, as we shall see, in a different way). But we must not be satisfied to stop there. New goals must be set that will demand more of the seminary than it has ever offered before (but note, the new structure provides more time to do it). To the goal of imparting knowledge, two more must be added—life and ministry. The student must be taught to turn knowledge into life and then into ministry; it is not enough to graduate men who are intellectually competent thinkers—they must be holy-living persons who are skilled in ministering truth to others in terms of their lives and ministries. The new, threefold emphasis of the seminary would be upon truth, growth, and skills; each of these would be thought important. All three would be inseparably related. Thought would be shown to lead to living and ministry; living and ministering would be shown to depend on truth, etc. The seminary would undertake, *in all that it does*, to train students to apply truth personally and in ministry to others.

Now, how are we to pursue these goals? A fresh approach to teaching and to curriculum will lay the basis for the change that will help to attain these goals.

Curriculum

First, let's take a look at the curriculum. I cannot develop a full curriculum in this article, and each seminary faculty and administration will want to do this on their own anyway. It will be necessary for them to sit down and do the following:

1. Define and describe the finished product that a seminary ought to produce.

Many seminaries don't even know what sort of person they ought to be graduating. When we don't know what we are aiming at, we are teaching in the blue. Teaching in the blue can be fun, and even interesting, but we deceive ourselves if we think this is the way to develop well-trained, properly equipped ministers whose lives are exemplary. Objectives should be clear and agreed upon by all (otherwise, there will be grit in the gears). Every faculty member should not only *know* what the graduate should look like, but should also know what he must contribute to that finished product and should be committed to doing so. *There is no place for dissension on this basic issue.* More concretely, the faculty should agree on the knowledge, lifestyle, and skills that a graduate should possess.

2. Define and describe the raw product that a seminary needs in order to produce that finished product.

Frankly, my impression is that many seminaries haven't the foggiest idea (apart from grade averages) about the qualities a seminary student should bring to the seminary (or how to evaluate a prospective student for them). Until this is decided, they will continue to accept unfit men who will be a grief to the seminary and to churches and who will, themselves, be miserable in the ministry. Once the seminary has defined and described the raw product in detail, it can structure the pre-seminary year to test for the requisite qualities and to develop them to a desired point prior to admission into seminary. The screening-out/screening-in process during that year can be the most useful feature of all for the seminary.

3. Define and develop a curriculum (and a methodology that is appropriate to it) that realistically will enable the seminary to move from that raw product to the finished product in three years.

One way to do so follows—again, only in sketchy form. Yet, it is an outworking of all that has preceded.

To begin with, stop departmentalizing the seminary. Departments tend to become little seminaries within the seminary; they are often clubs that have their own interests (rather than the total picture) in view. They tend to fracture the approach rather than integrate it. By all means, emphasize the specialties (development of peculiar gifts) of each faculty member, but minimize or (better) eliminate departments altogether.

In place of the departmental emphasis, structure the curriculum around the functions of the ministry. In this structure, all the valuable knowledge currently taught would still be taught, but not as the province of each department. Rather, there will be a new slant, a new stance in the teaching. All will be given an avowedly pastoral and ministerial focus. Everything taught now should continue to be taught, not as part of separate disciplines, but from the stance of life and ministry. Hebrew, for instance, will not be an academic discipline; it will be a way of understanding God's Word for one's own personal growth and in order to bless God's people. *All* that is taught must have the three goals (knowledge, life, and ministry) in view at all times. Teachers must teach, not in order to train other teachers, but to prepare men for ministry.

First, then, the faculty and administration (perhaps in conjunction with a number of key pastors and laymen) must define the functions of a minister of the Word (I can't do that here). Then, on this new curriculum structure, each faculty member brings his special perspectives to each function. This will tend to keep the focus on the *reasons* for teaching any given course. Those reasons will be based not on what the catalog says, or on how many hours a man ought to teach, etc., but on what a student needs for ministry. Thus, with these objectives clear about each function, both faculty members and students alike will be more likely to study with ministry on their minds.

Here is *one* way that this might be done. Let us say that we should divide pastoral functions into four broad areas of missions (including evangelism, home missions, foreign missions, etc.), edification (including preaching, teaching, Christian education, fellowship, etc.), administration, and worship (four broad areas in which a pastor ministers to his congregation). And, let us say, these would form the *basis* for the curriculum (that is, [1] everything taught would contribute to one or more of these areas; [2] everything would be taught *with a view to contributing* to them). Then, sections (and/or subsections) of each area would constitute distinct teaching units (or courses). Each section and subsection would be considered from the historical, exegetical, theological, apologetic, and practical perspectives of various faculty members in terms of knowledge, life, and ministry. There would tend to be more team teaching than now, but of a sort calculated to enhance rather than inhibit the work of both faculty and student. Specialties of faculty members would be integrated rather than departmentalized. The integrating factor would be purpose (of each course—recognized in ministerial function). Much more could be said here, but just so much for now.

Teaching

Also, as I said, we need new teaching goals and methods. As far as teachers are concerned, it will take young men (largely), with a vision for this sort of education, to staff such a seminary. Well-seasoned professors, formed by (and conformed to) more conventional patterns, on the whole, will not adapt well to this new approach. There will be some notable exceptions, of course. But not all younger men will do either; it will take flexible persons, committed fully to the basic concepts, to achieve what this program requires.

Secondly, professors should be pastorally experienced and oriented. They must not be men who have known nothing but the academic syndrome. Surely, one of the most serious problems seminaries have faced over the years is this gravitation of men who have no love for the pastoral ministry into seminary instruction.

Thirdly, the professors who are recruited for this new program should become models of what they teach, not merely models of someone talking about it. The discipleship methods (demonstration of theory; not theory in the abstract) *must* replace the Greek academic method (from the "academy"). Teaching, biblically speaking, is not merely *thinking* like one's teacher, but *becoming* like him (Luke 6:40). Discipleship is not an option; it is essential. It has an intratrinitarian base according to John 3,

5, 8, etc. Jesus *did* what He *saw* the Father *do* and *spoke* what He *heard* the Father *say*. If we keep His words, we will be His disciples as He is the disciple (apprentice) of His Father. Modeling is the discipleship method; showing (incarnated in a person doing it) what one speaks about.

Take, for example, exegesis. It is possible in any number of ways, for a student not only to learn the principles of exegesis (through reading and lectures), and to receive the results of his teacher's own exegesis. He also ought to be able to look over the teacher's shoulder to observe him *doing* exegesis. Then, in time, the professor ought to be able to look over the student's shoulder, too. Observation and supervision, questioning an expert in action, and guiding and correcting a beginner who is making his first efforts are essential elements of good discipleship teaching. What I have suggested for exegesis should happen also across the board for *every* subject.

Now, a few random words about teaching. What should be in view is competence in ministry, not grades in courses. The emphasis on grades in our schools has not had a salutary effect on students. There must be evaluation, of course, but I'll say a word about that in a minute. When we think about students with a B+ or C– mentality, something is drastically wrong. By emphasizing grades, schools have fostered fierce competition rather than loving cooperation. Students have been encouraged to work for grades rather than for understanding, retention, and competence. They have learned how to second-guess teachers' testing styles rather than learn information, lifestyles, and skills that will be important to ministry. What we want are competent ministers; what we get are test whizzers.

Criteria for competence ought to be established, of course. The faculty *must* give much thought to this. But, along these lines, at least one thing seems clear: a student must not be allowed to move on to the next learning opportunity until he becomes competent in what it is he must know, be, and do in order to assume that new responsibility for ministry. In other words, each competence must lay a foundation for the next. In evaluating competence, a significant part also ought to come from persons to whom he ministers, not merely from professors.

In gathering a faculty of the sort described above, there will be both opportunities and problems. At first, such a faculty will be built of younger men (for the most part), as I have said. They will be learning and earning degrees. They will not be well-known. But what they do can be supplemented by video-recorded materials by more conventionally oriented professors during the transition period.

Now, many questions arise. I would like to have taken more space to develop this article more fully, but this will have to do for the time being. I hope, however, that what I have written will stir some of you to thought and action. There is much at stake here; the time is late. I don't have all the answers, but I have given you a few, along with some general direction. Is there someone to whom you ought to speak about this matter, pastor? If so, make an appointment today!

Issues of the Heart

Today, there is a spreading acceptance of a concept that may fairly be termed *The Idolatrous View of Man*. To state what that means in the simplest way is to say that a man's (even a Christian man's) problems at the core may be reduced to one—idolatry. If one has a problem with lust, that is because his heart has set up an idol to lust after. If his problem is laziness, that sin stems from an "idol of laziness." Indeed, one proponent of this viewpoint was recently heard to attribute problems to a "sleep idol." Security, fame, work, family, money—you name it—may all become idols if one makes them so. Apart from the sheer reductionism involved, there would be little to quarrel with if that were all there is to this movement. Obviously, we all have problems with the tendency to put something/one in the place of God—and that is idolatry. But that isn't all there is to the matter. And therefore, it must be addressed.

What is the Heart?

Not feelings. The biblical view of "heart" differs radically from modern Western Valentine's Day ideas. Unwittingly, those who speak of preachers needing "more heart knowledge and less head knowledge" in their sermons do damage to the biblical view of the heart by this antithesis. They mean, of course, that preaching should not merely convey facts but, in addition, should present these enthusiastically by exhorting listeners to use them in life. That is a valid point, but speaking this way reveals that they have bought into an unbiblical way of thinking. To set the head (intellect) over against the heart (as feelings), however, is totally foreign—and contrary to—biblical thought. Nowhere in the Scriptures can you find such an antithesis. Indeed, biblical teaching forbids it.

"Well, if not by contrasting those two elements, then how should one express his thoughts about hypocrisy, etc?" Listen to the following verses:

> "*This people honors Me with their lips, but their heart is far from Me*" (Matthew 15:8).

> "*If you confess with your mouth, 'Jesus is Lord,' and believe in your heart that God raised Him from the dead, you will be saved*" (Romans 10:9).

> "*Who may stand in His holy place? He who has clean hands and a pure heart*' (Psalm 24:3,4).

> "*. . . man looks at the outward appearance, but God looks at the heart*" (I Samuel 16:7).

> "*The heart of the righteous considers how to answer, but the mouth of the wicked pours forth evil things*' (Proverbs 16:28).

> "*To man belongs the plans of his heart, but the response of his tongue comes from Yahweh* (Proverbs 16:1).

> "*Their hearts meditate on violence, and their lips talk about causing trouble*" (Proverbs 24:2).

And so it goes—*throughout* the Scriptures. Did you detect the common denominator in these quotations? In each, there is a contrast between the inner and the outer person to be sure. These were the antitheses: heart/lips; heart/mouth; heart/tongue; heart/hands; heart/outward appearance. The *external* is set over against the *internal* (heart). That—not head versus heart—is the biblical antithesis. You can see this antithesis plainly in 1 Peter 3:3, 4 where the writer contrasts the outer adorning of the body with the inner adorning of the *hidden person* of the heart. And it is expressly stated in II Corinthians 4:16 where Paul speaks of his outer person decaying, but his inner person receiving daily renewal of strength.

The biblical use of the word "heart" is large enough to encompass all that goes on inside a person. In Hebrews 4:12, for instance, God's Word is described as penetrating the inner person so as to judge even the *desires* and the *thoughts* of the heart." Indeed, throughout the Bible, "heart" is used to denote every possible activity of the inner person. No wonder the writer says, "Above all, guard your heart because it is the source of life" (Proverbs 4: 23). The word "heart" is often used when speaking comprehensively about the whole inner person, but also of the subsets of the inner person as well. For instance, the word "mind" is used to denote thinking and decision-making. The word "soul" is used synonymously with "life" since it refers to the spirit in conjunction with the body. "Spirit," in contrast, refers to the same non-material entity as "soul" does, but in its disembodied state. "Heart," then, encompasses all sub-sets when viewing the inner life of a person.[1]

Hidden—From Whom?

Peter, we noted, spoke of the "hidden person of the heart." From whom is it hidden? From man. God alone knows the heart. In Acts 1:24; 15:8) He is called the "Heart-Knower" because of this fact. Proverbs 21:2 says, "Every man is right in his own eyes, but Yahweh weighs the hearts." We also read that since "Sheol and Abaddon are known to Yahweh; how much more the hearts of the sons of man!" (Proverbs 15:11). And in Proverbs 17:3, we are assured that "God assays the hearts." God—not man—is the Assayer. According to Jeremiah 17:9, "The heart is more deceitful than all else, and is desperately sick." Then the question is raised, "Who can understand it?" Often, in quoting Jeremiah 17:9, the next verse is omitted. But God's own answer to His question is, "*I* the Lord search the heart, *I* test the mind [lit., the kidneys]."[2] See also Jeremiah 11:20; 20:12.

When Peter wrote about the "hidden person of the heart, then, he meant just that—one's heart is "hidden" from human view. If it is not

---
1 "Heart" does include the emotions. "Emotions" refers to bodily states; "feelings" to our perception of them. Thus, with reference to varying states of the body we say, "I feel sad, tired, elated, depressed" etc.
2 Considered the seat of the inner bodily states the perceptions of which we call feelings.

man from whom it is hidden, then from whom? Certainly not from God.[3] The simple conclusion is that *hearts are hidden from man*. For a human being to attempt to assay human hearts, therefore, is not only futile but also presumptuous. It is sheer folly: God—not man—is the Heart-Knower.

And when we are told that "man looks at the outer appearance, but God looks at the heart' (I Samuel 16:7), He is informing us about the fact that the latter is His province, not man's. Man can see and hear what others do and say, but only God can know what is truly in their hearts.

The apostle Paul waved aside the claims of anyone who would attempt to "judge" his inner motives with these words, "To me it is of little consequence to be judged by you or by the judgment of any other human being" (I Corinthians 4:3). He thought that such judging was worthless. Why? He continues, "indeed, I don't even judge myself." As well, he seems to have thought it impertinent to do so—in judging one's self (though, so far as he could tell, he had a clear conscience). But even about that, he suggested that might be wrong: "that doesn't mean that I am innocent." Then he said, "The One Who judges me is the Lord" (v. 4). The "purposes" of men's hearts cannot be known "ahead of time" (v. 5) because they are "now hidden in darkness" from the eyes of men (v. 5). They will be made known only when "the Lord comes." Indeed, Paul's comments make it clear that he thought it more than enough for one to try to look into his own heart, let alone into the hearts of others! It seems that Solomon had a similar difficulty. In despair, he cried out, "Who can say, 'I have cleansed my heart; I am free from my sin?'" (Proverbs 20:9). In summary, during Solomon's prayer at the dedication of the temple, he declared that *God alone* knows the heart (see II Chronicles 6:30; I Kings 8: 29). These two records of those words are conclusive.

A Misunderstood Passage

The phrase "Idols of the Heart" is said to be scriptural. Some proponents of the Idolatrous View of Man refer to Ezekiel 14. "Didn't Ezekiel

---

3 In contrast to the "hidden person [or qualities] of the heart" he sets the *himation* or "long flowing outer garment" (Souter's Lexicon) over against it. The one is hidden, the other is observable.

write about 'idols in the heart?' they ask. He most certainly did. But it is wrong to equate his language or his content with the contemporary view. Ezekiel did not use the words "idols *of* the heart." "Well," then, you may wonder, "Of what was he speaking and how must we interpret his words?" Three facts should be noted about the passage:
1. Ezekiel was speaking of physical idols—the gross idolatry of his day mentioned throughout his book.
2. His words have been misconstrued.
3. He was not setting forth a counseling construct as some think today.

Let's briefly consider each of these matters.

First, in his book, Ezekiel consistently wrote about the worship of graven images and other physical idols of his day that the Israelites had been worshipping. That is by no means the same thing as the worship of idols, which (allegedly) one has constructed for himself through the wickedness of his heart. How do we know that? Because throughout his book, what Ezekiel combats is always the worship of physical idols. In *every other passage* in His book this is so, and without clear reason to suppose the contrary, one *must* assume that here he does the same.

The purpose of the exile was to punish Israel for such idolatry and to rid them from it: "I shall scatter you among the nations, and I shall disperse you through the lands, and I shall consume your uncleanness from you." (Ezekiel 22: 15). The Jews were deported to Babylon to rid them of the idolatry by which they had polluted the land (See Ezekiel 20: 23, 24). Yet, instead of learning from this punishment and repentantly returning to Yahweh, they were so attached to their idols that they carried them into exile within their hearts (that is, in their memories). In this way, they continued in the idolatry against which Ezekiel preached.

Secondly, Ezekiel's words have been wrongly construed to teach that men *originate* idols in their hearts. That is not what Ezekiel described. The expression "idols of the heart" is not found in Ezekiel 14 (or, for that matter, elsewhere in Scriptures). The modern restatement of Ezekiel's "idols *in* the heart" has been subtly changed to the ambiguous "idols *of* the heart." The difference is significant. The modern view takes "idols *of* the heart" in an ablative sense to mean idols *coming from* a heart which *produced* them. But Ezekiel did not speak of the heart as the *source* of these idols. The original does not have the preposition "of." Instead, in Chapter 14, Ezekiel employed two other prepositions that do not mean "of." They are, respectively, "idols *toward* [or onto] the heart" (vv. 4, 7) and "idols *upon* the heart" (vv. 3, 4). The idea in both prepositions is that the idols have been taken into the heart from somewhere else rather than originating there.

Thirdly, Ezekiel wrote nothing about *searching* for idols in hearts. He already knew that the idols were present there. God, who searches men's hearts, had revealed this fact to him. The context of Ezekiel's words will not allow the modern interpretation (which, in fact, is a misinterpretation). The farthest thing from Ezekiel's mind was to provide a counseling construct by which one may discover and confront specific idols in counselees' hearts. To use Ezekiel 14 to support that idea is to foist it upon the passage. No one would have connected Ezekiel 14 with counseling if he were not looking for scriptural evidence to support his preconceived notions. As a matter of fact, it is not only in Ezekiel that such a counseling construct cannot be found; the same is true of all of Scripture.

The "stumbling block" mentioned in the context is the heart-borne idol. Rather than getting better, the situation is worse than before—idols are now placed right there "before their faces." Instead of having to go to temples or the high places to find an idol, those who have them in their hearts carry such images about with them. The temptation to sin was now even greater than before! As a consequence of this gross idolatry, God says that if an Israelite or foreigner inquires of His prophets, but separates himself from God through idolatry, he will be cut off and God's face will be against him (vv. 7, 8). God calls the people to repentance for this impertinence, declaring that *He* wants to take hold of their hearts for Himself.

In this brief excursus, I have attempted to set forth the fundamental problem with the modern view of the Idolatrous Man. That Paul calls "covetousness" or "greed" idolatry in Colossians 3:5 is not germane to the issue. "Why not, "you ask? Because of all of the matters that might possibly be thought of as idolatrous, covetousness *is* the setting up of something to worship that is greater to the individual than God.[4] But note, even then, Paul doesn't speak of "idols of the heart" but of idolatry in general. I suggest, therefore, that you avoid speaking of "the idol of..." in much the same way you would avoid referring to "the demon of..." Consider what has been said and distance yourself from any and all usurpation of God's rights as the Heart-Knower. Counselor, be satisfied with what you can know from what another says and does. His "outward appearance" alone is your God-given territory. God alone knows the heart!

---

[4] There is so much in man that does not fit the Idolatrous View. Sinful fear, worry, anger, depression and a whole host of other problems have little or nothing *per se* to do with idolatry.

Theology Today

INTRODUCTION: Some propositions to ponder:
- Every Problem is a theological problem
- Every Solution is a theological solution
- Every Christian is a theologian (good or bad)—whether he knows it or not
- Therefore, every believer ought to *study* theology.

The term "Systematic Theology" is in disrepute today. Certainly, we should expect this disdain from unbelievers, but sadly, it is also found in many believers as well. There is a kind of anti-intellectualism abroad that may best be expressed in the hackneyed back-woods preacher's phrase, "What we need is less theology, and more kneeology." There is, in some circles, also a strong dislike for the systematization of truth. As one such ecclesiastical detractor said to me, "I don't even believe in Systematics any longer; I think it's nothing more than rationalization."

At one time, theology was called "The Queen of the Sciences." (I've never been able to discover why the title "Queen" rather than "King" was used). But today," as Gordon H. Clark said in a lecture, "it is hardly considered a scullery maid." There are, of course, many reasons for this, but one of the most recent factors for its unseemly demotion is the current over-emphasis on "Biblical Theology."

Now, "Biblical Theology" is not what it may seem to be to the uninformed—a simple study of the Bible. It is, rather, the highly specialized term for a particular type of study of the Scriptures that has gained popularity among believers ever since Gerhardus Vos rescued it from the liberals. Some theologians have become so wrapped up in its interests that the study of systematic theology seems, to them, bland, uninviting. Even moralistic.

Why is this so? And how does Biblical Theology differ from Systematic Theology? The answer to the first question is easier to give than to the second. There is a newness to Biblical Theology which, because of its freshness on the theological scene, makes it exciting. There is new truth to be discovered and offered to a church "bogged down" in traditionalism (of which Systematic Theology has become the symbol for some). The "discoveries" are, however, in dispute among biblical theologians themselves making, for many, an exciting field for internecine controversy. In academic circles, this polite conflict, in itself, can be pleasant and, when handled improperly, can lead to the following of groups of otherwise theologically uninformed students.

What is Biblical Theology? There are several things held in common among the many differences found among those who pursue this task. Principal of these, perhaps, is the goal of finding Jesus Christ in the whole of the Scriptures. The phrase "The History of Redemption" frequently occurs in the corpus of such writings. Possibly, these two factors alone tie all conservative Biblical Theologians together as they seek to find redemptive nuances in unexpected places, particularly in the Old Testament. In the process, they differ greatly in the major themes, types, and other seeming indications of the big picture presented in Scriptures. In doing so, the reader is often asked to accept connections that are only apparent to the writer and are questionable to the reader. Moreover, in this big picture of redemption as it is forecast in all of the Scriptures, the pastor is often left in a quandary. Should he ever use a biblical passage in an exemplary fashion (as Paul seems to have done in I Corinthians 10), or must he, too, somehow find the nuances that seem hidden except to many of the experts? Some Biblical Theologians claim that to preach in an exemplary manner is to do damage to the text, and even to deny the Lord Jesus Christ. Yet, they must explain away Paul's use in order to do so.

In considering the "History of Redemption," the big picture often becomes everything. The individual, in his endeavors to serve the Lord, is forgotten. We must remember that Christ is the subject of the Bible; He is all. True. But is there nothing to say to the parent struggling with disobedient children? Is the mere mention of Jesus Christ and His redemptive work enough to help? What of the Christian wanting to know how to honor his Lord at work, or at school? Is there nothing practical to tell him? Is practical preaching—that never leaves Christ out of the picture—really moralism? Given these matters, isn't it time to debunk many of these theoretical constructions that hardly agree with the practicality of Proverbs or the Epistles? Well, yes, and no.

What is a proper view of Biblical Theology? To the extent that it has legitimacy at all, we must properly accord to all of redemptive history the two-fold character of Genesis 50:20, where Joseph saw both the big and the smaller picture in perfect harmony with one another when he said to his brothers,

> *You meant it to me for evil, but God meant it to me for good, and that He might save a people alive.*

God was concerned about Joseph as an individual when He led him providentially through many difficult experiences. But he was equally concerned about saving the people of Israel through Joseph, since it was out of that nation that the Messiah would come. There is no need to divorce the one from another. Indeed, to make Biblical Theology one's sole interest is to neglect the everyday Christian faced with his everyday trials and tasks. I have taken the time to discuss this issue because, somewhere along the line, it is likely that you will encounter issues having to do with it, and it is well to be informed.

Now, back to Systematic Theology. The process of culling all that one can from various parts of the Bible in order to determine what the Bible has to say about any given matter is not an easy but a difficult task. That is one reason why Systematic Theology is important—apart from a systematic understanding of the Bible, in which one determines all that is said about prayer, for instance, one may be led astray by reading only one or two passages on prayer that seem to tell him he will receive all that he prays for. When he does, and he fails to obtain his wishes, he may become confused or discouraged. A systematic study of prayer will tell us what to pray for, how to pray for it, what the conditions are under which to pray for it, and when and when not you will receive a positive response from God. Those are, of course, only a few of the aspects of prayer that are covered in an exhaustive study of the subject. But you can see, from this brief example, how important systematic theology is. So, one studies the subject in order to be accurate in his understanding and his living for God.

The attempt to encompass *all* God has said about *any* subject has as its goal, not the puffing up of one by knowledge, but the ability to properly love God and one's neighbor. One who is astute in his knowledge of the Bible knows that truth brings about godliness (Titus 1:1). The opposite is also true: error leads to ungodly living. So, the study of what God is like, what man is like, what God has done, and what He requires of us is a worthy effort that ought to be made by every believer.

Such systematic study is possible because God and His Word are understandable with His help (I Corinthians 2); biblical truth is systematically self-consistent (the one mind of the Spirit is behind all of it); all truth is one (even as, in contrast, error is manifold; see I Thessalonians 5:22). Theology is the skewer that makes sense out of life by organizing and arranging and applying otherwise scattered truth.

Theology is practical for living since it relates truth to man's problems and points to God's solutions.

How should it be studied? One must learn theology by comparing Scripture with Scripture in order to clarify and grasp the fullness of any given truth. To do this, he uses the tools of exegesis (how to obtain from a passage what God intended the reader to obtain, without addition or subtraction). As I have said, one must compile all passages pertinent to a doctrine in their relationships to one another. In this way, he obtains a complete and, therefore, accurate understanding of God's truth.

The main areas of doctrine that are usually comprehended in the study of Systematic theology are the Bible's doctrines (the word means "teachings") about

1. Scripture (Bibliology)
2. God (Theology proper)
3. Man (Anthropology)
4. Sin (Hamartiology)

5. Salvation (Soteriology)
6. Church (Ecclesiology)
7. Future (Eschatology)

In and of themselves, it is unimportant to know the technical terms for each area of doctrine, but as a matter of reference I have mentioned them. Frequently, in the reading of Christian literature, you will encounter such terminology, so it's good to have a place to reference its meaning.

Too few "Christian" laymen are prepared theologically. They may have a Ph.D. in some subject, but only a Sunday School degree in Bible. Thus they find that they don't know what to believe or do in any situation where they need to systematically apply God's truth to their lives. Instead of a rapid response, they themselves stumble in the use of truth, or give wrong advice to others.

Twisting Scripture is frequent in modern Christian circles. Many think that they know enough to advise others, when the truth of the matter is that they distort God's Word because they are (as Peter put it) "untaught" and "unstable" (II Peter 3:16). A proper understanding of Systematic Theology, as much as anything else, tends to forestall such error.

How important it is, then, to be conversant with Theology rather than to ramble through the Scriptures in a slipshod manner.

On Writing

There are people who have a lot more going for them than they realize. I think that many of the graduates of Westminster Seminary, both those who are graduating this year and those who have graduated in years before, are among those people. And it is just because you who are gathered here as alumni may have a lot more going for you than you yourselves would admit, that I'd like to talk about one way that Westminster graduates have failed to develop their full potential.

Let me make one thing clear as I begin—I'm not supposed to preach to you tonight. I'm not even going to take a text. I was told I could talk about anything under the sun that I wanted—that I could lecture, tell jokes, or do almost anything. So I decided to speak about something I have never talked about before. I don't know if I'll get anywhere with it or not. My theme is writing.

While it isn't true that all Westminster men have failed to realize their writing potential, I believe that in this room tonight, just from looking around, there is the possibility of producing reams of good material that could be sent out in this country and around this world to make a tremendous impact. And because that hasn't yet happened, I'd like to talk to you about that possibility a little bit tonight. I'm not doing so because I think that I can say a great deal that will be helpful, but perhaps just bringing up the subject could be the most helpful thing that I can do.

You know, of course, that the Reformation was not just a preaching enterprise. Preaching was very central to it, but accompanying the spoken word were the printing press and the writings it produced. The Reformers used that press to the fullest. In God's providence, the Reformation was spread by the printed page, perhaps equally as powerfully as by the pulpit.

If we intend to propagate the Reformed faith with power in our day, we must get it out there in print in a hundred different ways—in bulletins, in tracts, in pamphlets, in booklets, in books, in magazines. Wherever the opportunity exists and you can move the printed word into it, is a potential area for a powerful ministry!

You who are about to graduate have been writing for three years; some of you four, some five! We've given you all the practice anybody could ever need—term paper after term paper, exam after exam, writing, writing, writing. We professors go back home with piles of papers in our hands, loaded down with written material that *you* produced. But suddenly, a man leaves the Seminary and he stops writing! That's a tragedy. It ought not to happen, and it need not do so. I call on you to continue to write.

Now, what could I say to encourage you to write, and what sort of offhand suggestions could I make to somehow or other trigger a few ideas for you? First of all, you will really write only when you have some purpose for doing so. You must have a significant, burning purpose in view. I don't think you'll write unless you do. Some people will, of course. There are people who will write, just as there are some people who will preach, without a purpose. I have asked a preacher, "What were you trying to do in that sermon?" And he'll say, "What do you mean, what was I trying to do? I was preaching." And then I'd reply, "Yes, but what were you hoping to accomplish by your preaching?" He can't answer because he doesn't have any purpose in mind. His only purpose was to fill that block of time that preachers have to fill twice a week on Sunday. He thinks, "I'm getting up to preach, that's my purpose." If that's the only purpose a man has when he gets up to preach, he's in sad shape. He should know so clearly what his purpose is that he could give it to anyone, any time, on a moment's notice. He should know so clearly what that general purpose is that if you were to roll him over on Sunday morning at three o'clock and say, "What's your general purpose in the morning message today?" he could spit it out in one line. Then, when he goes back to sleep again, you roll him over once more and say, "What's your specific purpose?" and he can nail that out in one line without even batting an eyelash and go right back to sleep again and not miss a snore.

Unless a man knows what he intends to do to that congregation in a given message, he isn't preaching.

The same is true of writing. If you haven't got anything significant to say, of course, there's not much sense in writing. But when you do get something down inside that begins to work away at you, you should think about committing it to writing. You start to get concerned. Something begins to gnaw. It gets to you. You can't even sit down at the table and eat without it intruding into the pie. You wake up in the morning an hour or two early and your mind is racing around thinking about that same subject. You relax with your feet up and it's the first thing that comes into your mind. When this happens, I think you'd better start writing. Otherwise, you'll never get to sleep, and you won't enjoy your pie. If God has put a burden on your heart for something, you ought to write about it. Start delivering that burden both in the pulpit and in writing. So, first you need a significant purpose. You need to know what you intend to do when you write. You will know when it is significant if you watch for your burdens.

Now, sometimes you've got a purpose clearly enough, but you think, "I haven't quite got the courage to put that down in print." It does take a little courage to put some things in print. You know, what you say audibly, even with all the tape recordings we have today, tends to evaporate more quickly. But what you put down in print, even if it gets balled up, mashed together, and thrown in the corner, has a way of coming to light again. Someone can always get hold of that little wad of paper and open it up and read it again. And then somebody else, and somebody else—you can't ever quite get away from it.

It is also true that those who read may not agree with it. They may disagree radically. But if you're fairly sure about what you have to say, if you know that it comes from the Word of God, that God wants this said, and that there are many people who need to hear it, a lot more than those who can hear your voice, you had better get it down on paper whether all of the consequences are pleasant or not.

I had a real struggle at one point on this question over the book *Competent to Counsel*, which some of you may have heard about here or there. When that was in mimeograph form, I sent it out to a number of people—Don Tweedy, Bruce Narramore, and a half dozen other people. They had about two months to read it. Then we all met together in a motel for two days, and they told me what they thought of it, which was a very interesting experience. (I'll never forget that two-day period down at the Airport Motel in Philadelphia.) It was an interesting experience from a lot of angles, but the one thing I want to mention is this: to a man, in effect, they all said, "Even if it's right, it's too rough. Don't publish it like that; smooth it out. People will be upset. Take the edge off of it." You know, that troubled me. I went home and I thought and prayed about what they said, and I became concerned about that matter. I thought about their writings and reread some of them. I concluded, "They're too soft. They don't have *enough* rough edges. Maybe that's why they haven't done anything earthshaking in this field." So I went home and I sharpened it up more!

But it does take a little bit of decision making and courage at points to decide what it is that you're going to produce, because they are right—not everybody is going to like what you write, especially when it involves a new departure. But you see, if you're really burdened with God's Word, it has to be said. If it's getting into your pie, if it's getting into your sleep, if it's getting into your relaxation period, you've got to do something about it. You can't stop eating pie. You've got to get the thing off your chest and onto paper and out there where it can do some good. And I think there are a lot of you who have things on your chest. You often talk to me about those things. You're concerned about those things. You'd like to see a lot of things changed. I never talk for two minutes with a pastor or a graduate or somebody who is about to graduate from the school, it seems, that he isn't concerned about changing something. Well, great! Most of those concerns are legitimate. But let's **do** something about them, not just talk to each other! Let's really get out there in print and talk to the people who need to hear about it, and maybe something will happen.

The second thing I'd like to suggest is that when you write, it should not only be because you have a significant purpose that pushes itself out, but it should also be for the benefit of the reader. You see, you can go too far in the other direction. You can only think of the benefit of the writer. What you can get out of it in the way of notoriety, or what you can get out of it in the way of funds, or simply what you can get out of it in the way of release of tension. You can go too far in this business of saying, "I've just got to get it in print, because I've got to say this thing. I've got to get it off my chest." If it's only a matter of making you feel better, and not really being concerned about the person who needs to hear what you say, that's wrong.

Writers who become all wrapped up in some kind of esoteric group where those on the outside can't understand what they are talking about are not concerned about their readers. Their ideas are restricted to some small coterie of people who can worship the writer, who himself makes it clear that he isn't sure they truly understand either. When one's followers write commentaries that disagree with one another over what the leader has to say, it has gone too far. I don't think there should be any Christian writing like that. This kind of esoterica often grows out of confusion, either in the writer or in his writing. Either his thinking isn't straight, or he doesn't know how to put it down straight on paper. There isn't any subject that can't be discussed clearly in writing. The most profound subject can be made very simple and clear. Oh, I know the danger. I've had people tell me I'm simplistic when I write clearly. But I've spent many, many years working on the problem of writing clearly.

Ever since the time when I took work with Andrew Blackwood and he made us turn in our papers in a form that would be perfect for publication, I've been concerned about writing. We hated it! But we learned from it. He insisted not only on good form but clarity! Over the years I've come to believe that clarity is very close to truth and that obscurity is very close to lying. And I'm thoroughly convinced that many people whose writings are obscure want to be obscure because they're afraid to be clear.

I don't think any man who writes obscurely about God's truth has a reason to do so. The Lord Jesus Christ was not obscure, yet He was the most profound Person who ever lived. He was clear. He was explicit; far too explicit for the Pharisees. He was shocking to His relatives and friends and very plainly assuring to those whom He forgave. He left no one in confusion except when He spoke in parables that He wanted only certain people to understand. There isn't any subject, if we care to be clear about it and work at being clear, that we can't make clear, no matter how complex!

One of the ways to hinder clarity is by using jargon. Preachers are terribly guilty of using jargon. I sent some men in our first year preaching course this year out on the streets to talk about their sermons to people who did not know Jesus Christ as their Savior. Some of them were shocked that they would have to do such a thing to begin with, but others learned some very valuable lessons out of this experience, they told me. One of the things I read again and again in their reports was this: "I realized that I couldn't communicate with a person who didn't know my language, my biblical language, my theological language, my jargon. People would say, 'Wait a minute, what are you saying?' " So they found that they had to step it down; they couldn't use the high voltage of the Seminary. They had to bring it down so that it wouldn't burn out all the appliances in the home. In other words, they had to make themselves clear! (Incidentally, one student even got somebody to come and hear him preach at the Seminary.)

But you see, that's one of our modern tragedies. We steep ourselves in books filled with jargon. Then we begin to speak and write using the same jargon and perpetuate it. We don't need a special language. Oh, among ourselves at school it's very good; technical language is an excellent shortcut. In our churches, among the leaders, you can use certain terms. To understand the Scriptures, we have to learn the key terms. But I'm not talking about those things particularly. I'm talking about all the unnecessary jargon that we build into our preaching. It is the sort of jargon that doesn't communicate but just turns people off.

I'm calling you to write, but I'm also saying let's start writing English. Let's start using English that approximates the fish-market Greek in which the New Testament was written. There was a literary kind of Greek that was around that could have been used, but it isn't in the New Testament. Instead, God chose the simple Greek that every man can understand. That's what we'd better start using when we write. Use the New Testament writers as your example.

Thirdly, if we really care about benefiting our readers, we're going to be very much concerned about reader analysis. We're going to want to know all about their needs and knowledge. We're going to want to really know where they are. We're going to want to meet those needs through clearly stated scriptural answers. You can't obscure the gospel as I've heard it obscured by men, and really meet the needs of sinners who need to know that Jesus Christ came into this world to die for guilty persons. You've got to make it clear. That gospel has to be made explicit. Paul said, when he was talking about the gospel, that he minced no words and made it very simple; he said, "I determine not to know anything among you except Jesus Christ and Him crucified." He said, "This is the gospel that I preach to you … how that Christ died for our sins according to the Scriptures and was buried and rose again on the third day according to the Scriptures."

That is so simple; there is nothing complex, nothing esoteric. It is simple enough that the little schoolboy who really hasn't learned very much in his ghetto education can understand it as well as a seminary professor. Everybody needs to be able to understand the gospel and the teaching of the Bible in any walk or condition of life. God in the Bible made it clear, but we have obscured it.

When we talk and write, if we wish to be intelligible in form and in content, we also need to be sure that we have a style that is unique. That's what really makes a difference, cultivating a communication style. Now you can go overboard in either direction. Your style can be so much like everybody else's that there is no style, or it can be so different that nobody can understand it. But style really means uniqueness within the commonalities! And that's what we have to cultivate—a way of saying things into our community and into our age that rattles the windows in people's homes, that shakes their beds, and gets them concerned. That takes some work. And you know, this whole business of style is something that we need to think a lot about, because style is not something you can buy tomorrow at the store; it's something that you already have. Realizing this is like the fellow who went to college and suddenly realized that all of his life he had been speaking prose. You don't get a style tomorrow, you've got one! The first time you opened your mouth or wrote something on a page, you had a style. The only question about your style is whether it's good or bad, whether it communicates or doesn't, or whether it's frozen or flexible, whether it's green and growing or dead. Those are the kinds of questions you need to ask. You've got one. What's it like? Do you even know?

One more suggestion. I know you want to be perfect. You want all your written material to be just so. Somebody, you fear, may find a comma in the wrong place and misunderstand you. But if you want it all to be so perfect, you'll never write anything. That's why a lot of you don't write. Probably the key reason why most of the people in this room don't write is because they say, "It's gotta be perfect if I write it." If everything had to be completely perfect, I doubt that Calvin's *Institutes* would have been written. He began with publishing more or less of a pamphlet that grew and grew. You've got to put something out if you've got a burden, and do your best where you are today. Improve tomorrow as people criticize. Criticize it yourself, but keep at it until you get to the place where you begin to communicate. Your work will never be perfect anyway; that's why you'll never publish anything if you wait for that.

But, last of all, what you write has to be true to God. You really have to be sure that what you write, as far as you can tell, grows out of that basic commitment to the Word of God, that revealed Word which He has given to you. And the commitment must be that, "I shall never write anything on a page of paper unless I, to the best of my knowledge and ability, am convinced that I have checked this thoroughly by the Word of God." That must be your rock-ribbed philosophy of writing. If you adhere to it, it will put spine into everything you write.

Well, I think that's about what I want to say tonight. I still hold the record at these meetings set ten years ago for the shortest address ever given, and I want to live up to that model. I think there are two things that need to be said about one of these addresses. Either one of these two things can make an address here worthwhile: it can be brilliant or it can be brief. And since I have no hope of the former, I'll sit down now.

Influence[1]

I don't want these concluding remarks to be merely parting words; I want them to be instructive. In one way or another, the claim has been made that nouthetic counselors do not believe in the importance of outside influences upon our counselees. Let me say it here, and say it clearly—I believe very firmly in the importance of influence! The influence of parents upon children is colossal; the influence of peers is sometimes overwhelming. I don't think that anybody who believes in 1 Corinthians 15:33 can deny the importance of influence. So let me take my stand here and now with those who believe that the Bible teaches that parents and others can (indeed, will and therefore ought to) influence their children, and that counselors ought to influence their counselees.

But certainly, while I believe in the tremendous power of influence, I must disbelieve those who say that its power is so great that there is no greater power that can overcome it. That view is, in reality, disbelief in the power of influence. It denies the possibility of a counselor to more strongly influence those who are being or who have been influenced. That's really what the Bible teaches: that no matter how powerful the influence of parents and peers and others may be—and it is powerful—God's influence is much more powerful. I do want to maximize the power of Jesus Christ to overcome any and all influences that He cares to. That is what the gospel and the sanctifying power of the Holy Spirit are all about!

So much for the possibility and the power of influence. That's not what I want to talk to you about today. Rather, I want to talk about some

---

[1] Adapted from Dr. Adams' closing remarks to the second annual conference of the National Association of Nouthetic Counselors (NANC) in 1977.

of the sinful influences that are at work in your lives and mine. Counselors too, must recognize the power and possibility of influence—adverse influence—on themselves and their counseling theories and practices, and must guard against it.

A very significant passage in the last two verses of 1 Timothy 6 addresses the question of influence. There, Paul says to Timothy,

> *Timothy, guard that which was entrusted to you, turning away from the irreligious chatter and contradictions of what is falsely labeled 'knowledge,' which some claim to have, but by taking poor aim have missed the target of the faith.*

That passage, I think, says something of significance to us as counselors. Of course, Paul is not speaking directly about counseling. His interest is much broader than that. He sets forth the principles by which any Christian minister, in particular, or any Christian worker, in general, might handle false, erroneous, and misleading influence of any sort, involving any aspect of his ministry for Jesus Christ.

But from that broader background, I'd like to focus only on that one aspect of it, an aspect that is included and that we're concerned about in this meeting. On the other hand, we must remember the other adverse influences brought to bear upon us as Christian workers. Let's think, then, about the influences that move against us in counseling and how we may follow the admonitions given in this passage to keep us from being wrongly influenced. The influencing power of Jesus Christ that can do this for us comes through the Word as it is used by the Spirit of God who inspired it.

Now notice first, in verse 20, that Paul urges Timothy to" guard"—to *guard what God gave him*. He must guard that which was "entrusted" to him, Paul says. That is a very interesting exhortation. God has given to us a deposit of information. It, of course, centers around and flows out of the Good News, the gospel of Jesus Christ; but it branches out into all the implications of that gospel, all the out workings of that gospel in Christian life as they are explained in a book like 1 Timothy. What he is talking about is those things that he has been reminding Timothy about all through this book. He is also talking about the things that he enlarges upon in the second letter to Timothy(and of course in Titus and the other books of the New Testament that tell us what God has entrusted to workers in the Christian church).

Principally, in this passage (and the pastorals), he speaks to Timothy as a minister of the Lord Jesus Christ; one who must not only preach those truths and faithfully model them as a man of God, but also one who is called on to guard those truths that are revealed in the Scriptures.

In one way or another, people would try to pervert, eliminate, or add to what is in the Scriptures. This will be the nature of the influence exerted on Timothy; and it is against allowing such influence to prevail that Timothy is warned. This is Satan's ploy: he always attempts to affect God's Word so that it becomes of no effect. From the very beginning, Satan's aim was to cast doubt upon the Word of God, a doubt that leads to a denial of the Word of God, and then to defiance of that Word of God. That's how he usually progresses: he casts doubt that leads people to deny certain truths and then leads them in their lives to defy what God has taught in the Scriptures. You can see that process at work in Genesis 3. You've already preached about it I am sure; I don't have to reiterate it for you.

But this scriptural deposit has been given to you (literally, "put by your side as a trust from God"). God handed it over to you and expects you, in turn, to hand it over in bright, shiny, well-kept, and well-preserved form with no missing pieces, without additions, and unwarped. Your job, and mine, is to preserve that gospel trust. So, to begin with, we have to realize that this is one of the prime tasks of a minister.

In 2 Timothy 1:12, a verse that we all know by heart, Paul again talks about something that was entrusted. Literally, he says, "He is able to guard my deposit against that day." We have a hymn that says, "He is able to keep that which I have committed unto Him against that day." There is truth in that hymn, but that isn't what the passage means. That passage is wrongly interpreted, because of the wrong translation of the King James Version. Paul is not speaking about what he had entrusted to God but about what God had entrusted to him. The Greek says literally, as I have pointed out, "my deposit." He is able to preserve my deposit against that day.

Now a deposit can be called "my deposit" from two different viewpoints. You go up to a window, and there's a bank teller behind the window, and you make a deposit. Now that's *your deposit* when you lay it down on the counter to the bank teller. As a depositor, you may speak of "my deposit." But if you're the bank teller sitting behind the window, the minute that the depositor's money has been entrusted to you, it becomes *your deposit*. And you—as the teller—also may think of that deposit now as "my deposit" because you are going to be held responsible for it to the depositor and to the bank. You must guard that deposit. Because the person came to your window, you are held responsible for it. It was entrusted to you; it's your deposit. If there is something missing from it at the end of the day, they start searching for it; nobody can go home until the figures balance. If they find out that you put it in your pocket or didn't take care of it, you are in trouble. The context shows that the words "my deposit" refer not to the person putting something into the window, but the opposite. Paul is thinking of himself as the teller who received from God, who made the gospel deposit with him, a sacred trust.

This runs throughout these letters to Timothy. Cf. 1:14 where he writes "Guard the good deposit entrusted to you through the Holy Spirit who dwells within us." That good deposit was entrusted to Timothy, and this emphasis continues in chapter two of 2 Timothy, verse 2, "The things that you heard from me before many witnesses, pass along to the trustworthy persons who will be competent to teach others also." Paul pictured this good news of the Word of God handed on as a sacred deposit from one trustworthy person to another. God entrusted His Word to people who must be trustworthy in preserving it, guarding it, and passing it on. That's the picture.

Now God, Himself, is at work in that process. The wonderful thing is that it is *God* who keeps or guards it against that day. *We* are told to guard it, but God says that *He* will guard it; the same word is used in both passages. We are told to guard it, but God will guard it; that's not a contradiction—it's a wonderful truth. That is what I was talking about last night, and I want to reemphasize here: there is a dual responsibility. You and I are held responsible for guarding the deposit, but we are held responsible for guarding it *in God's way*, not in *our way*. A teller might say about a deposit made to him, "I'm going to guard it by putting it in my wallet and taking it home and keeping it at my house." Well, he won't get away with that, because the bank has decided how he is to process and guard the deposits that become his responsibility. He must do everything in a prescribed manner. He can't keep his own personal records or put the money in his wallet; he must use the bank's recording system, and the deposit eventually must get into the vault. His personal responsibility is to follow the bank's procedures; he hasn't any right to make the decision about how to guard a deposit.

Likewise, neither you nor I have the right to decide how we will guard the deposit that God has given to us. He has deposited it with us; He has told us to guard it, but He also has told us how to guard it. And just as the bank teller guards the deposit by depending upon the bank's procedures and powers to do so, we too must guard our deposit in God's strength, by following His Word.

We must guard the deposit through the Holy Spirit's power working to help us understand what the Bible says about guarding it, and then obediently following what the Bible says. You can't guard God's deposit in your own strength any more than a bank teller could guard his. You don't guard God's deposit by your own wisdom. You guard God's deposit by biblical methods and by the Holy Spirit's strength. The two responsibilities fall together. God is responsible for giving you the deposit, telling you how to guard it, and giving you the strength to guard it. You are responsible for following and obeying His instructions.

What are these instructions? The first thing God tells us about guarding the deposit so that we may pass it on unharmed is "Turn away." Now that is a very interesting exhortation. "Turn away!" he says, from the influences that would diminish, add to, or twist that deposit of truth and faith that is in the Scriptures, once for all given to the saints. You must turn away from all adverse influences. That certainly means that you do not guard God's deposit by getting deeply involved in that which is wrong. Rather, you must turn away from it. Bank tellers can't hobnob with crooks and use their methods!

I had planned this talk long before I came here, and I had no idea what Henry Brandt was going to say, but I was extremely interested in his emphasis upon not getting yourselves involved in a lot of psychological and psychiatric study. And he demonstrated that he practices what he preaches in everything that he said here. He didn't turn to any of that sort of material. He depended entirely on the Scriptures. Now there are a lot of people who think that they can guard the deposit of God by getting all wrapped up in that which is erroneous. I don't know how they can think that way. I don't know how they can reason that way, but I know one thing: God says it isn't going to happen. You won't guard the deposit if you do that. Instead, you will let down your guard. To guard the deposit of God, one must turn from all that which would chip away at, dilute, or pollute biblical truth. You have to maintain a certain kind of distance from it. Wherever you recognize or identify such influences, you must hold out your hands and say, "Wait a minute. I don't want to get involved in this."

This exhortation doesn't mean that you don't need to understand something of these influences; it doesn't mean that you don't study them enough to know that they are harmful influences, or what the enemy is going to do. Paul was able to talk about the enemy; John was able to talk about the enemy. Paul said, "We are aware of the wiles of the devil." John talked about gnosticism in his letters, and understood and refuted it thoroughly. This doesn't mean that you don't become acquainted with bad influences, but that you don't side with them.[2] Henry said so well, in speaking about Psalm 1, that you don't walk in the counsel of the ungodly. You don't allow yourself to be influenced by it. That's what turning away means.

Further, let me note, turning away means that you can't be involved in two ways: first, in *accepting* false beliefs, and secondly, in being caught up in *continual argumentation* with those who propagate false beliefs. Notice what it says: "Turn away from the irreligious chatter and contradictions of what is falsely labeled 'knowledge.'" There is a vanity and an emptiness about error. It is called, "irreligious chatter." I don't know, for instance, why anyone who believes the Word of God should take training in T.A.

---

2   Of course, under the intention of studying, one may become so involved that he gets caught up in that in an unhealthy way.

He can pick up enough books on it to read what he needs to know to warn his people and refute it in contexts that might be profitable in winning somebody from it. But to get involved in courses in this, actually sitting around the table learning the vocabulary of the irreligious chatter of this new form of Freudianism with emphasis adapted by Berne from Erikson and passed down to Steiner and Harris, violates this verse. T.A. admittedly has very clever packaging, lots of good publicity, and uses catchy expressions. But it's the old ego, superego, and id under the new names of parent, adult, and child. In his chapter on values in *I'm Okay, You're Okay*, Harris reveals a viewpoint that is anti-biblical from the word "go." Turn to the chapter on values in which he says that "truth is a continuing progressive on-going kind of thing. It is not found within the pages of a black book." You know what black book he had in mind. He wasn't talking about the telephone directory; he was talking about the Bible, and he was saying truth is not found within its covers. Now any system that has that as its fundamental principle about truth is anti-Christian.

I can see studying T.A. deeply enough to warn people about it, but I can't see doing anything but turning away from its beliefs and its practices and its principles. That's what Paul is talking about in this passage. There is a time to turn away. This is not scriptural obscurantism. We don't wear biblical blinders on our eyes so that we don't know what's going on. No, the Bible wants us to know everything that's going on around us. Paul, at Athens, could quote from the enemy's sources and turn them back on them; but while we don't turn away from understanding and learning about false systems, we do turn away from their influence. This is what Paul is saying.

There is something very important here. Paul speaks not only about what such influences are going to do to your counseling, but also how they affect you. Let me make that point clear. Counseling has to do with living. It has to do with how you evaluate and meet life situations. It has to do with how people live at home, how they live with their wives and children, how they live with other people, and how they live with God. That's what counseling is all about: attitudes, values, beliefs, and behavior. Since that's so, what you become involved in day after day, where you put your major emphasis, where your thoughts are continually moving, the kinds of practices and the kinds of principles that you become committed to will influence your *living*. I've often thought about Christians who have become involved in some theory like Rogerianism as the deep emphasis of their whole life's work. Rogerianism is a theory of living; that's exactly what it is. It is a theory that teaches that man is totally capable of handling his own problems by his inner resources. Rogerian non-directive practice conforms to this theory. Rogers bases this theory on the presupposition that man, at the core of his being, is essentially good. Now that kind of unscriptural thinking and practice (in which you never speak with authority and you never use God's Word to tell counselees what to do) influences the counselor and his way of life too. It has a tremendous impact on the life of the counselor. You can't live with that kind of theory of life and follow the kinds of practices that grow out of that theory day after day without affecting your home life, your personal life, your social life, and your life with God. It is very dangerous to allow ungodly influences to have free play in our lives. Rogerian autonomy ultimately leads to a kind of rebelliousness toward God and His Word and undercuts the authority of God's Word in one's life. Talk to a Rogerian who has been into it for years and years, even though he is a Christian, and you will see that his view of Scripture has been influenced. He may proclaim allegiance to the Bible, but when you observe his practices and listen to his viewpoint, you can easily detect the influence. The same is true about Freudian excuse-making (always finding the problem in somebody else). You will discover that the counselor who has been deeply involved in it will, in time, begin to excuse his own behavior. You can't avoid the influence of what you believe and practice on your own life. And, of course, it also makes an impact on the deposit that God has called you to guard.

Osmosis does take place. You know what osmosis is? It's the passage of a liquid or a fluid through a semi-permeable membrane, the direction of the flow always being from the less dense to the more dense substance. And when you continually live in such an anti-Christian atmosphere, it will get through no matter how dense your substance might be! It's going to get through. Take it as a warning, because this personal warning is what Paul was talking about in verse 21—how persons in the places of leadership may be influenced. Influence has caused people not only to lose, to minimize, to defile and to pollute that great and glorious deposit that God has given to them, but they themselves, "by taking such poor aim" about the goals of their lives and their ministry, "have missed the target of the faith." They have veered off from proper ministerial directions and goals.

The third thing that we have to realize from this passage is that there is a way of recognizing such influences in spite of the fact that there can be a problem with identification. At the outset, we must recognize that there often is a problem in identifying erroneous influences that are at work on us. We often do not even realize that they are there. Paul says that these influences are falsely labeled "knowledge." Many things that look good and sound good actually go under false labels. They fly under false colors. They are attractively packaged, but the packaging is misleading. The color combinations will have been thought through carefully according to motivation research standards. The same soap put in three different colored boxes sells differently. Color experts put some soap in a box that was all blue. The women said, "It doesn't do the job; it doesn't get the dirt out." They put the very same soap in a box that was yellow, and the women said," It's too strong! It ruins our hands and the items we put in." They put the same soap in a third box, which was blue with splashes of yellow, and the women said, "It's wonderful!" You can influence by packaging.

Labels, too, can influence. Paul makes that clear when he says "falsely called" or "falsely labeled knowledge." You could almost put garbage into a beautiful box and sell it! Look at the label Paul warns about: "Knowledge." Who doesn't want knowledge? Knowledge! We've found it at last! Eureka! Paul says that this use of the word is a pseudonym. Our English word pseudonym comes from the Greek word used here, "to falsely call or label something." "Knowledge" is often a false label, a pseudonym, Paul says. But what an attractive name it is. It's the name that the devil put on the fruit in the beginning. And that has been the problem all the way through. Most have thought they could find knowledge somewhere else than where God said it is. Man thought he could find knowledge on his own. That was Satan's clever misrepresentation. Anything labeled "knowledge" is an appeal to you and me just as it was to Adam and Eve. "Here's the latest knowledge! Here's the latest scientific knowledge. "These words appeal. The counselor can say, "I'm on the in. I've learned special esoteric knowledge with great Greek and Latin words attached to it that sound impressive." (Such knowledge usually has a lot of mule words that begin with Greek and end with Latin.) The appeal, in part, is, "If I could just get hold of what these words mean, I'd know so much more." But so often it's nothing more than the devil's age-old appeal.

NANC is still a puny little organization. We haven't even filled all the seats in this room. This is a puny organization. Who wants to be part of a puny organization? You could join an organization that has thousands of members, power, and prestige, and you can talk in jargon. That's knowledge. You see, people have to make decisions. Where does real knowledge lie? Does it lie in what is widely labeled knowledge, or does it lie in what's inside the package? It's your job not to be deceived by labels. If you're going to lead other people out of the traps of false packaging and misleading advertising and all that goes along with it in this field of counseling, you're going to have to become astute in going beyond the package and the advertising to analyze the product, so that you can warn others (and to avoid it yourself).

This isn't always so easy. That's why Paul has to talk about it here and has to point out that much is falsely labeled knowledge. Satan comes as an angel of light, and you will hear all kinds of groups, organizations, and viewpoints say, "We have new light on the subject." Scripture talks about Satan, the angel of *light*. Have you ever thought what that meant? Light in the Bible is the symbol for purity, truth, and holiness. But it is also a symbol for *knowledge*. Satan still comes as an angel of knowledge, as he did in Eden; as an angel who can give you new light, new information, new insight, new methods, all these new things; light! You were walking in darkness; now T.A. comes along. You were walking in darkness; now P.E.T. comes along. All our homes and schools will be revolutionized by P.E.T. Sure, there will be revolution. But in what direction?

Today the argument runs, of course, that all truth is God's truth. Truth appears in any and all of these different systems; not just out of the Bible, but out of all Freudian, Rogerian, and other systems as well. And this happens, allegedly, by the common grace of God (that's the other catch phrase—watch out for these catch phrases, for these cliches). "God's truth," we are assured, and "The common grace of God works in all men and even unbelievers who are given much truth that we can learn from." That's the advertising out among Christians today. That's the kind of packaging we see everywhere. Is it true?

Well, all truth is God's truth. Who would deny that? That's like saying, "Mothers produce babies and apple pies." Sure they do, but those statements are used in a context where they don't fit. Freudianism and all its anti-biblical views and practices are taught on the basis that, "You can't abandon them, because all truth is God's truth, in the common grace of God, and certainly there must be a lot of truth here." But that doesn't follow. All truth is God's truth, but we must be careful to discern which "truths" are those truths that are God's truths. And the way we find out is by the Bible. We don't just take something as true because somebody says, "There must be truth in Rogerianism." There is some truth in Rogerianism, bent so out of shape that we can't use it. The truth that comes from these groups may grow out of a Judeo-Christian background in which the people were reared, and their values or morals were influenced to some extent by this; but it has been so distorted or perverted and so twisted within the framework and methodology of the system that it can't be used. The place to find truth about living is not in Freudianism, but in the Bible! And, as Brandt said so well, if you have to go to the Bible to find out what's right elsewhere in the twisted mess, you might just as well start with the Bible. That saves an awful lot of heartache and trouble. Now, in the common grace of God, unbelievers do develop many good things, but you see, we are working in a different area from medicine, engineering, etc.; don't let people deceive you.

People say, "You claim the Bible as a textbook for counseling. Why don't you use the Bible as a textbook for engineering? Or medicine? Or for a hundred other disciplines? Why do you say the Bible is the textbook for counseling?"

"Well," I say to them, "I don't use the Bible as a textbook for medicine, because that wasn't the purpose for which it was given. I don't use the

Bible as a textbook for engineering because that wasn't the purpose for which the Bible was given, either. The only reason that I use the Bible as a textbook for counseling is because that is the purpose for which it was given. And it had better be used as the textbook for the purpose for which it was given." You can't set up other textbooks as rivals in a competitive fashion and have them fit the Bible. And when people say about those things, "This comes from the common grace of God; this is God's truth because all truth is God's truth," they miss this critical point: *the Bible was given to tell us how to live.* The Bible tells us how to love God and how to love our neighbor. So when you come to the areas of truth, values, behavior, attitude, and personal relationships, when you come to areas like these, you do not need to turn anywhere else; indeed, you *dare* not turn anywhere else for your principles. In this book are "all things necessary for life and godliness." *All* things. You either believe that or not. If you don't believe it, you dare not call yourself a biblical counselor.

Now is all this anti-intellectualism? No, just the opposite. You are called to use the intellect God gave you to sharply distinguish truth from error. The antiintellectual is the one who doesn't make the effort to discover what the Bible says and then develop practices that grow out of biblical principles that are in harmony with it. He is content to ride the easy way as a consumer of manufactured products. He never starts with the flour, water, salt, and yeast; that's too hard. He wants the pre-packaged stuff that is already mixed; you just add some water and you have instant this or that. Look around and see who has done the *hard* intellectual work. It is the people who have tried to be radically biblical. They've had to go back and dig and scratch and work hard at it. The people who have taken a package of T.A. mixed thinly with misapplied Scripture in an unholy mixture, and poured it out on a pan to harden, *they* are the ones who have avoided the hard intellectual work. That doesn't satisfy Paul's words in this passage. It is anti-intellectual to drift the easy way. There is still much hard work that needs to be done, intellectual work, using the minds God gave us to discover in this book a thousand things that we haven't even thought about yet. You men who are involved in it know that you must work. It is not an easy job; and so much yet needs to be done.

I like that passage in Philippians 1:10 that instructs us to discriminate between the things that differ. How easy it is not to do that hard work of discriminating. According to the original Greek, to do so requires testing. One does not merely accept something on the basis of its labeling. It's so easy to say (as so many people do), "Oh, you're dealing with reward and punishment and behavior, so you're just Skinnerian. You're Christian behavior modification people." Listen, God talked about behavior, reward and punishment, long before the behavior modificationists came on the scene. But people so readily and easily identify behaviorist practices and principles with biblical reward and punishment principles of behavior modification, because they don't take time to discover the differences between the two. They see the same words and practices (in some respects) that look alike and identify the two, failing to recognize that they are greatly different all along the line.

Let's take an example. Dobson's *Dare to Discipline* has sold well in evangelical circles. Why? First, because of excellent packaging. It has first-rate labeling—the title hardly could be better. It came at a time of reaction, when people wanted to hear (and needed to hear) that children could be and should be disciplined. Its labeling is a tremendous selling point; but when you get inside the package, what do you find? Testing shows it to be Skinnerian behaviorism. The product is mislabeled. This is not *biblical* discipline. When you train a child by that method, you're training him in the modern day methods of behavior modification, not in the kind of behavior modification and discipline that the Bible talks about. The child is trained to avoid that pinch on his shoulder muscle. That's what he's trained to avoid. And if you continually follow up wrong behavior (according to behavior modification principles) with the adversive control (punishment) or with the reward for the right behavior, what are you training a child to do? You're training him to look for the immediate gratification of his desires and to avoid immediate pain. That, in my opinion, is to train him in criminal behavior. Fortunately, human beings are more than animals. The principle behind it (whether Dobson realizes it or not; I don't think he does; he's probably a fine Christian who bought this thing hook, line, and sinker) is that man is only an animal. That's the fundamental Skinnerian principle. And the principle behind it is operable, whether the person using it is a Christian or a pagan, because that is what Skinnerian methods are calculated to do: train a person the way you train your dog. It may be fine to train your dog that way. It's not so fine, however, to train a human being that way.

Both Ephesians 6:4 and Proverbs look at discipline quite differently. Proverbs talks about the rod, *but it also talks about reproof* (Prov. 29:15). And if you study the use of the word reproof carefully through Proverbs, you find that it is equated with *instruction* and verbal confrontation. So, Proverbs advocates discipline with the rod (reward/punishment) and with reproof (verbal confrontation). And what we find in Ephesians 6:4 also stresses both sides together. We read not only about discipline by reward and punishment (nurture) but also about nouthetic confrontation (admonition). The two must be held in balance; otherwise discipline becomes something quite distinct from biblical discipline.

This is the kind of thing that we dare not soak up by osmosis, thinking all the while that we're really disciplining our children biblically by using only a reward/ punishment structure. If we don't also confront our children about the gospel of the Lord Jesus Christ (the other side of the Ephesians 6:4 and Proverbs 29 coin), we fail miserably. We must talk to them about coming to know Christ as their Savior. Then, once they have come to know Christ, we must urge them to obey and serve out of gratitude and love for Him; not just in order to get rewards or to avoid punishment. Discipline must move from that to the desire to please God. Man is not only an animal; he has been created in the image of God as a moral being who can sustain a relationship with God. In shoulder pinching, you miss all the theology the Bible teaches about man and Christ, and you adopt something that looks and sounds biblical because it talks about discipline and reward; but in reality, the two are miles apart.

When you talk about the gratification of the immediate reward and the avoidance of the *immediate* pain, you forget that the Bible talks about the *eternal* reward and *eternal* pain. So unless you talk about immediate reward and immediate punishment *in light* of the eternal context, you can't even discuss immediate rewards and punishments properly. Those eternal facts condition all temporal rewards and punishments. But such a view of reward or punishment is no longer Skinnerian, because Skinner doesn't believe in eternity. And so you see, things that differ must be distinguished. Much, much more could be said about that.

"Anti-intellectual," they say? What is anti-intellectual? To accept claims that something is biblical, to accept packaging and advertising claims that aren't substantiated by testing the product itself.

There are two kinds of knowledge according to Genesis 3, and there are two kinds of knowledge according to I Corinthians 1 and 2. The intellectually honest thing to do after careful discrimination by the use of the biblical standard of what is true and what isn't, is to turn away from that which is not. Test all things and hold fast to that which is good.

Now, let us ask, what characteristics does such false knowledge have that you might be able to identify it? The answer to this important question is also in the passage. *Kenophonia* is the first characteristic. This Greek word used in 1 Timothy 6:20 and 21, means empty talk, irreligious chatter, something that looks good on the surface, but once tested, examined, and analyzed, proves to be empty and hollow. It does not meet its claims. It claims that there is *something more* that you need, but it really has nothing more to offer; that's the essence of it. Claiming to offer something more, so much of the writing of psychology is written in very pompous-sounding jargon. But when you closely examine a term like psychosis or schizophrenia, you find that there's really nothing to it, because there are any number of widely differing views about what the word means.

Carl Menninger said a couple of years ago, "Schizophrenia? That, to me is just a nice Greek word." That's so often where you end up. But you must do the work of discovering whether there is something to the claim or whether there isn't. So many empty words in counseling sound as if they refer to substance at first, but within they are hollow. Watch out for claims of something beyond your Bible in counseling. Anybody who offers you something "beyond" your Bible ought immediately to be suspect.

The other word here, translated "contradictions" in the New Testament in everyday English is literally, in the Greek, *antithesis*. It is the same as our English word carried over from the Greek word. These are contradictory claims, opposing opinions, competitive concepts. Whereas the first characteristic of views falsely called knowledge is that they fall apart when you examine them because they are really empty and hollow and don't offer something more, the second characteristic is that they offer *something different* from what the Bible says. Something more; something different. These are the two claims to be alert to. If you can get a person to believe that he needs something more, it won't be long before you can tell him something different. That's the way things moved in Genesis 3. "You need something more," said the snake. When they were convinced of that, they were told, "Look, here's something different that is really truer." That's what you have to watch out for. What's so amusingly sad is that Christians have failed to see the competitive nature of opposing views. They fail to recognize the theology of Skinnerianism, the theology in what Rogers is saying, and the theology of Freudian psychotherapy. These are not indifferent neutral viewpoints. When Skinner says that man is only an animal, he's stating a theological viewpoint about man that differs radically from the biblical view. Its implications are vast. When Rogers says that man is essentially good at the core of his being, and that he doesn't need an authority or power from outside, that's also a theological viewpoint, and so on.1 We must recognize the *theologically competitive nature* of these views, and that, in fact, they are posed in antithesis to biblical teaching. They are influences competing with the deposit that God has told us to guard.

Competitive viewpoints, concepts, or principles, turned into practices, in a subtle way undermine Christian convictions because they are designed to produce ends that are competitive to the Bible; that's the way that God's deposit is eroded. By the introduction of these antithetical concepts - little ones here, little ones there - brought in along with disjunctive methodologies here and there, Scripture is soon displaced. Watch out for this! Avoid not only whatever claims to be an addition to the Bible, but also whatever claims, "Here is a better way of doing it." If that "better way" isn't based on and doesn't grow out of biblical principle, avoid it like the plague.

If you don't understand, just think about this: every counseling system is out to change people's patterns of living. And every system that wants to do so without God's power or without Scripture's directions is competitive.

"If you don't believe me," says Paul, "look at the example of what has happened to those who have done it." Those who have allowed themselves to be influenced, who have let down their guard, who have not turned away, who have not learned to discern between things that differ, and who do not recognize the two characteristics of that which is falsely labeled knowledge, have gotten into serious trouble. He says in verse 21, "Some claim to have knowledge, but by taking poor aim, have missed the target of the faith" (i.e., the very thing that they were given - the deposit - the faith entrusted to them). As Jude says, it was "once for all deposited with the saints." "Learn from their example," says Paul, "look around you. Open your eyes. Look at what has happened to people who have been thus influenced."

When they missed that goal, it happened by setting up other targets toward which they aimed their efforts. You, too, should take a look at people who started out in the gospel ministry who have turned aside. I know about dozens of them. Some were once very fine preachers of the Word of God. Yet, somewhere (meaning well, wanting to help others), they became involved in psychological counseling, and their goals began to shift from transforming men's lives by the gospel, and the sanctification of believers by the Word of God and the power of the Holy Spirit, to other goals. Under the influence of these other systems, they set up new targets other than those which are laid down in Scripture. Thus they missed the faith not only for their counselees, but for themselves, because they were distracted by new targets. They began to claim, "We have more knowledge," but the claim soon fell by the fact that they soon turned away from the preaching of the Word. They began to psychologize rather than exegete the Word, and in many instances they forsook the preaching and teaching ministry of the Word and are now doing psychological work exclusively under their own shingle. You've all seen that happen. I don't have to tell you about it, I just need to *remind* you of it. There isn't a man or woman in this room who couldn't name five cases that you know like that. "Don't think it couldn't happen to you," says Paul; and he says this to *us*.

"What do you do then, when"—that's been the theme of this conference, "What to do when." Well, "what do you do when an ungodly influence is exerted on you?" Let me sum up Paul's answer to that question. (I) Recognize the influence for what it is by testing it according to scriptural criteria. (2) When you see that it is ungodly, and that if followed it could wean away from you the deposit that God has put into your safekeeping, hang onto and guard that deposit with your life. (3) Turn away from that false teaching rather than becoming involved in it, and (4) instead of professing to have this kind of knowledge, and propagating it, and getting involved in it and promoting it as so many do, turn your back on it as you (5) remember what it did to others who became involved.

May God bless you and make each one of you strong and stalwart guardians of His Word, to believe in it, to teach from it, and to counsel by it. That is what will keep NANC doing God's will, and only that. May God grant that it never turns from that purpose. The minute it does, I personally will turn away from it.

www.ingramcontent.com/pod-product-compliance
Lightning Source LLC
Chambersburg PA
CBHW060532100426
42743CB00009B/1504